THE MEAT & POTATOES GUIDE TO

INSPECTED · APPROVED

BUSINESS SURVIVAL

THE MEAT & POTATOES GUIDE TO

BUSINESS SURVIVAL

A HANDBOOK FOR
NON-MBA'S & COLLEGE DROPOUTS

. . . .

ED BASLER

Published by Advantage, Charleston, South Carolina.
Member of Advantage Media Group.

ADVANTAGE is a registered trademark and the Advantage colophon is a trademark of Advantage Media Group, Inc.

Printed in the United States of America.

ISBN: 978-1-59932-486-9
LCCN: 2014956796

Book design by George Stevens.
Author photo by Dev Photography—Chicago.

This publication is designed to provide accurate and authoritative information in regard to the subject matter covered. It is sold with the understanding that the publisher is not engaged in rendering legal, accounting, or other professional services. If legal advice or other expert assistance is required, the services of a competent professional person should be sought.

Advantage Media Group is proud to be a part of the Tree Neutral® program. Tree Neutral offsets the number of trees consumed in the production and printing of this book by taking proactive steps such as planting trees in direct proportion to the number of trees used to print books. To learn more about Tree Neutral, please visit www.treeneutral.com. To learn more about Advantage's commitment to being a responsible steward of the environment, please visit www.advantagefamily.com/green

Advantage Media Group is a publisher of business, self-improvement, and professional development books and online learning. We help entrepreneurs, business leaders, and professionals share their Stories, Passion, and Knowledge to help others Learn & Grow. Do you have a manuscript or book idea that you would like us to consider for publishing? Please visit advantagefamily.com or call 1.866.775.1696.

To my children, Julian, Charlene, Joanne, and Hayley

To my grandchildren, Joseph and Julia,
and the grandchildren to come

To my sons-in-law, Justin and Elias

And to my loving wife, Cathi, who supports us all …

Onward and upward!

TABLE OF CONTENTS

ACKNOWLEDGMENTS

I have enjoyed a lifetime surrounded and influenced by friends, visionaries, and business owners.

I want to express my appreciation to my mentors, including Wedge and Shirley Alman, who are two of the most amazing people I have ever known;

> Berne Bertsche, an inspiring visionary and entrepreneur;
>
> Bob Weiner, who is Mr. Faith and Vision;
>
> Jon Pritiken, who is Mr. Strength;
>
> and
>
> Joe Bobb, Rod Biedler, Dawson Trotman, Yarli Nino,
>
> Chuck Porta, Bruce Leckie, Melody Green, Ari and Shira Sorko-Ram,
>
> Eitan Shishkoff, Chuck Schumacher, and Stu Heywood.

Thank you also to my family mentors: my mom, Helen; my dad, Erv; and my great siblings Adrienne, Dennis, and Brian.

To my best friends who keep me accountable and make me laugh: insurance guru extraordinaire and fellow Brother of Thunder biker Robert P. Burnett; real estate guru and fellow Brother of Thunder biker Bruce Utterback; and Scott Tidwell. Special thanks to Robert Sheasley, my editor.

And I want to honor the memory of two great men of God who will be forever missed: Joseph Manahan and Ronald Juran.

ABOUT THE AUTHOR

Ed Basler is a longtime entrepreneur and CEO of E.J. Basler Co., a company that provides precision-machined parts and solutions to companies all over the world. He is also a sought-after motivational speaker and President of Fresh Eyes Coaching, a firm that helps small businesses identify profit opportunities and obstacles. Ed and his wife, Cathi, also founded and ran a nationally recognized not-for-profit youth organization for 15 years. The couple has four children, two sons-in-law, and two grandchildren (so far). They live in the Chicago area.

For more information about E.J. Basler Co., go to
www.ejbasler.com

For details about Fresh Eyes Consulting, go to
www.fresheyescoaching.com

....

SUCCESS WITHOUT AN MBA

Long ago I was sitting in a business management class at a Wisconsin university known for its business school. I was a freshman and I thought, "This is great. I get to grow, as an entrepreneur, and learn real life business principles."

This was not to be. Sad to say, after attending four weeks of classes, I realized that the professor had no real-life experience in running a business. Somehow, at the ripe old age of 18, and as the son of a business owner, I had managed to obtain more hands-on experience and knowledge of business management than my professor.

As I sat in the hot and stuffy Old Main classroom, listening to the instructor drone on and on, all I could think about was the clock on the wall and why it was running so painfully slowly.

I knew early on in my college career that I was on my way out. I felt my enthusiasm and motivation deflate week after week as I listened to theories that were of no relevance to me. The professor had gone to school to learn theories that he could just rattle off to us, and once I learned he lacked any real business experience, I didn't feel very motivated to listen to much he had to say. He wasn't providing a lot of practical examples his students would find useful in their coming careers. It just seemed like book knowledge.

I couldn't connect the dots on how this would be valuable to me—more valuable, that is, than the business experience I already had gained, and what I had witnessed at my father's manufacturing company.

I am a simple and practical guy, and I saw little in the way of common-sense advice. When you know more than your professor, you find it hard to concentrate, which leads to big trouble academically. Two years later, I dropped out (or rather, was kicked out) of my business management path and came back to "Sweet Home Chicago."

But the entrepreneurial fires were just beginning.

THE BEST TEACHER IS EXPERIENCE

I used to feel bad when I was with friends who had their MBAs and other degrees, but I soon realized that the majority of people who run businesses and succeed do not have an MBA and haven't even graduated from college. Some of the most successful people I know and some of the most successful people in history barely finished high school or dropped out of college. Bill Gates, Steve Jobs, Mark Zuckerberg, Walt Disney, Ray Kroc, and Richard Branson, to name a few, never finished college.

In Appendix 1, you will see that I have listed quite a few more names.

You see, no matter what the business is, the best teacher is experience. I did get my degree. It was from the college of hard knocks. Yes, I do read the *Harvard Business Review* and also try to keep up with the books written by the brightest and best, but when I look back, experience has counted most. It has been my teacher. I have learned by doing, and that is how I have matured as a businessman. I have always been a hands-on person. Just show me how to do it, and I want to do it.

I decided that I would enter my career path head-on and face life and the world and stop throwing money away on a degree when, instead, I could be pulling money in. I'd had numerous jobs in the real world, and I couldn't see the value at that time of spending any more time in college just to say I had a degree.

So, I went right into business and started working with my father. As soon as I left college, I immediately joined him in the machining business he had founded, and then, on the side, I also dabbled in the small businesses I had started.

WHY START OUT WITH A BURDEN?

Do not get me wrong. I believe in education and learning, and there is nothing wrong with an MBA or a college degree, but it also disturbs me to see young people coming out of college with tens of thousands of dollars of debt, particularly when I read that 54 percent of recent college grads have no job. And if you get your MBA, your total setback can be $100,000 to $200,000 when you figure in room, board, tuition, credit card bills, and the value of the annual wages you did not earn because you were pursuing that degree.

That is quite a burden for a young person to carry while starting out—and all this before even picking up the first paycheck. How long do you think it takes somebody to finally pay off the debt and the interest? It is insanity. I think there is a better way to succeed.

Laszlo Bock, the senior vice president of people operations who is in charge of hiring at Google, related this in a (6/19/13) interview with Adam Bryant in *The New York Times*: "When you look at people who do not go to school and make their way in the world, those are exceptional human beings. And we should do everything we can to find those people." He also observed that "too many colleges do not deliver on what they promise. You generate a ton of debt. You do not learn the most useful things for your life. It is [just] an extended adolescence."

A SERIAL ENTREPRENEUR

I am a serial entrepreneur. At present, I am the chief executive officer of E. J. Basler Co. (www.ejbasler.com), the company my father founded. It is a Chicago-area manufacturing company that is a strategic supplier of precision-machined component parts that go into everything from autos to tractors to hydraulic assemblies to plumbing to aerospace. Our parts are in products people use every day all over the world. I am also the president of Fresh Eyes Coaching, a firm that helps small businesses identify profit opportunities and obstacles.

I love starting businesses. I love the challenge of succeeding in a competitive market. I have started and run many businesses including a used-car rental agency, a coffee shop, a music venue, a 10-minute oil-change service, a manufacturing company, a consultancy, and a wedding dress boutique.

It is my nature is to be an entrepreneur. Most entrepreneurs are pioneers, myself included. I like to explore new territories. I like something fresh, something new. I find the challenge exciting. I was in the used-car rental business because that industry was brand new, and business just boomed. I had read an article in the *Wall Street Journal* that this was the up-and-coming thing, and it was, for many, many years.

Same thing with the 10-minute oil change. That was a brand-new concept and I jumped on it. And the wedding dress boutique was a venture that I undertook with my wife, who is also a pioneer and entrepreneur who has operated businesses on the side, even to this day. The boutique, called Catherine Simms, was the first retail store to return to the downtown area of Arlington Heights, Illinois. It was rather depressed at the time, and today it is thriving. We were the first to show a renewed confidence in that area. It was a very successful adventure for us.

I have looked for opportunities wherever they might arise. You must not limit yourself. How do you find opportunities? I think you have to just look for trends. In every generation there have been so many opportunities. Look at what generations past have experienced, from the dawn of the Industrial Revolution to the age of the automobile and aviation. This march of progress has not stopped, and so many have tapped the potential in the informational and technological revolutions.

I recently visited the Harley-Davidson Museum in Milwaukee. When you walk through that museum, you see Harley-Davidson was founded as a bicycle shop in a garage. Then, they decided to put motors on their bicycles, and the rest is history. Sometimes it is a small idea, but if you just stick with it and look for opportunities, you may well see it grow.

You can be an entrepreneur by launching into your own business, but you can also bring the entrepreneurial spirit to an existing enterprise, even a large company. For example, Harley-Davidson's progress, every step of the way, has been driven by someone coming in with a new idea, with an entrepreneurial thought. In fact, the company recently introduced an electric motorcycle. Whether devotees will miss that renowned "vroom" remains to be seen, but you never know. You have to have the thought before it can count.

LEADERSHIP AS A MISSION

For 15 years my wife, Cathi, and I ran Souled Out, a not-for-profit youth organization. My wife and I always had a heart for young people, especially those who were on the fringe and who had come from difficult backgrounds or broken homes. After working with Vietnamese boat people, orphanages, and foster care, we ended up adopting a 14-year-old boy from Romania. With three daughters at home, this changed our family completely. We knew that in order to make this adoption successful and get him to blend in with our family, we would have to be alert to his needs as well as those of our own children. This boy was a people magnet, and with his sports buddies and friends from school, we had teenagers over at our home all the time. We began an open door policy and our home became the place to be.

My wife was very proactive in keeping the young teens busy and when we started planning sports activities for them, we began to have meetings in our home as well, talking about tough subjects and spending time connecting with all of them. It wasn't long before our home was overrun with teenagers. We would have up to 70 people show up in one week. So, we took the meetings out of our home by buying a building. We developed a not-for-profit youth organization that ended up attracting hundreds of young people every week. We ran a coffee house, a music venue, and a weekly meeting that encouraged young people to make a difference in their society. In the summers, we took youth to several different countries to open their eyes to the world around them, giving them opportunities to grow, serve, and lead in many cultural and international settings.

We had a vision to teach these children the strength of positive peer pressure and trained them in leadership. We had them lead the meetings that we held in our coffeehouse, managing everything from the music to the speaking. They ran a coffee bar and started a dance troupe, as well as working on a music team. These young people put out three music CDs. We worked with the poor in Chicago and neighboring suburbs. We worked a lot with the Salvation Army. We sought out opportunities for young people to go to other countries so they could serve in other cultures and acquire a world vision. Young people went to Haiti. They helped with the problems caused by Hurricane Katrina. They went to Africa, and to many other countries. Throughout the years, many of these young people traveled to over 16 different nations. When some of the leaders were away in the summer, we formed a whole new team of leaders who continued the work at home. The coffeehouse also saw teenagers coming weekly from 15 different high schools in our area, and some would travel for over an hour to get there. We even began sister work in a small college town in Iowa, with a different group of young people.

Our leadership training syllabus often took the leadership principles of author John Maxwell and author and youth leader Ted Stump. We would spend a week discussing each of the principles. During those weeks, we would give these kids opportunities to hold a small discussion group in their homes. Each group had a leader and an assistant leader, and when a group grew to more than 12 people, the assistant leader would start a group with six of them and get his own assistant. That way, we had a constant flow of young leaders for the organization.

These years were very successful and very full. Finally, after 15 years, when our own children had grown up and moved on, and when funding had dried up, we closed what had been a very successful youth organization. Today, these former young leaders are now parents and leaders in their own right. Some have become very successful. Many of them have gone into international work. Some of them are in the public eye. Our adopted son is now a gymnastics coach and owner of several gyms, happily married and influencing a whole new generation of young people in a positive way. Our daughters graduated college. Each of them spent time studying internationally for her degree. Several of the young people who were part of our group are now business owners or leaders in the area. From the activities of the little group that began in our living room with our adopted boy, all our children have developed lifelong friends from all around the world—not only our children, but hundreds of others too, and all are better off from their connection with our youth organization.

It was deeply fulfilling to see so many young people embrace leadership and to see their lives touched and changed. That is a mission I hope to continue with this book, in which I share the lessons of leadership I have learned in my life as an entrepreneur.

A LESSON FOR THE YOUNG

In working with young people, I often emphasized the importance of vision and of the value of job experience. I'd tell these kids, "Hey, rather than sit at home or bemoan the fact that you do not have a job, go to McDonald's. McDonald's is always hiring, and it is a fabulous opportunity to learn one of the best management systems in the world." They would be involved in one of the most successful franchises and business models of all time. What a great place to learn!

I talked with many young people who thought the job would be beneath their dignity. I told them they were not just getting paid to flip hamburgers but were actually being paid to learn a management and customer service system that has successfully been introduced into almost every country and culture. This was accomplished through training people who have very little educational experience and turning them into team and business leaders.

As they slap on that secret sauce and turn over the fries in the deep fryer, they are learning something fundamental. They are learning teamwork, cooperation, and efficiency. They are learning the ingredients for success.

I have been all over the world, and the McDonald's franchises are reliably similar in how they are run. A young person can learn so much, whether it is being accountable with the cash drawer, or even the importance of just showing up punctually every day. I can see that the job is intense. You've got to be on your A-game at the drive-up window, or at the counter, and get the food out superfast or else customers get upset. The McDonald's system is inspiring. In fact, if someone gave me the opportunity to work at McDonald's, I'd probably take it for a week, just to see how things are done there.

That is how much I value experience, and that is the lesson young people need to grasp. So, go ahead and flip that burger, but also keep your eyes open and look around you. Look at what the boss is doing, and the managers, and each of your coworkers, and ask questions.

I have learned from each of my endeavors. Through each of them, I became stronger, as a businessman, and made fewer mistakes. Henry Ford said, "Failure is only the opportunity to begin again, this time more intelligently." As I often would tell my wife, the mistakes and lessons I learned in those businesses were still cheaper than an MBA. Today I am still learning in the best of all schools: the school of experience.

FATHERLY INSPIRATION

I learned a lot from my dad, Erv. When he was five, his father, Joseph, died in the 1918 Spanish influenza epidemic in Chicago, along with over 8,500 other poor souls. At an early age, my father had to learn how to be the man of the house and the breadwinner. His story inspired me. He was a first-generation immigrant who struggled through the Great Depression, but he had the entrepreneurial spirit. He ran a small machine shop that made parts for mighty John Deere and International Harvester tractors and engines.

My brothers and sister and I strived to gain our father's approval. He was a hard worker and expected us to be the same, so from the age of eight, I earned money the old-fashioned way. I delivered papers for the Chicago Daily News for five years. I started my own landscaping and snow removal business at age 10. I learned early on that an entrepreneurial spirit could make money and also serve the needs of the neighborhood.

My dad worked till the day he died of Lou Gehrig's disease at the age of 78. I never heard him complain of too much work. Like many people in the Depression era, he had a remarkable work ethic, which he instilled in his children. He believed if you weren't working, you were lazy. We weren't sitting around

watching TV in our house. If he saw us sitting around, he'd put us to work with projects around the house, and also, on the weekends, he'd take us to his factory and we'd work in the shipping department, packing parts, or we would sweep floors.

I eventually took over my father's business, and it has qua-drupled in size. Our new goal is to double in size within the next five years. Right now, we are at $23 million in sales. We are going to double that in five years, and we have put in place the necessary training to accomplish that ambitious goal, as I will explain later.

YOU CAN MAKE IT

The Meat and Potatoes Guide is a generous serving of good, sound, nourishing advice. It contains business principles and practices, simply put for regular folks who dream of running a business.

Statistics show that for the average business start-up, the failure rate is 8 out of 10 within the first 18 months, as reported in Forbes magazine—meaning, 80 percent of start-ups do not make it even that long. I want you to be in the 20 percent who do make it.

I have never attended, it seems, a business seminar at which non-MBAs have spoken. The speakers have always been consul-tants and "experts" who often have not actually run a business. Yet they profess to tell people what to do. How refreshing it would be if the speakers were to include entrepreneurs, no matter what their education levels or list of credentials were.

This book is the product of 40 years' experience in running retail, service, manufacturing, and not-for-profit start-ups. Through failures and lots of successes, through economic upturns and downturns, I have learned how to beat the odds and rise above the competition. I will show you how to be not only a survivor but also a profitable winner in whatever business you are in. The principles are universal and will work for any business in any country for people of any educational level.

TIME FOR YOUR MEAT AND POTATOES

What I offer you here is not a four-course dinner at a fancy MBA restaurant. This is not a get-rich-quick formula. This is not a two-year, tech start-up miracle. This is not sushi, foie gras, or caviar. This is meat and potatoes, a meal we all love and can afford.

The Meat and Potatoes Guide presents lessons learned and paid for on the front lines and in the trenches of everyday small business. These are lessons that can be easily digested by any man, woman, and student who has the heart of an entrepreneur and who is smart and willing to work hard to achieve a dream.

It is time to pass the plate and dig in.

"If you can dream it, you can do it."

WALT DISNEY

(who succeeded without a degree)

C H A P T E R   1

....

THE POWER OF VISION

Vision: Something seen otherwise than by ordinary sight; something beheld as in a dream; a visual image without corporal presence; an object of imagination; power or activity of the imagination; unusual foresight.

I have started many businesses, but all of them began with a vision, usually a consuming grand vision of what they could and would become. Successful pursuits begin with the germ of an idea that grows into a vision of how that idea will unfold. If you can't see it, it won't happen.

I always thought I had big vision. Not only was my father a visionary but my mother also showed me what real vision was.

After my father died, my mother, who was younger, moved back to her childhood hometown of Decorah, Iowa, one of the prettiest small towns in North America. A small but grand hotel once graced the middle of the town, hosting many special events. It had a beautiful lobby with ornate stone floors and a three-story atrium and stained glass.

Like a lot of hotels in small-town America, it eventually went out of business. It became a rundown boarding house, and a second-hand shop opened where dignitaries once strolled the lobby.

Next to it had been a grand opera house, but it had been abandoned. The walls were covered with graffiti, the windows were broken, and rats scurried amid the debris. But my mother remembered its glory days. She had a vision of it once again becoming a proud member of the community and even grander than it was before.

I will never forget the first time she took me for a tour. At best, I thought, it was a teardown. I could not imagine in my wildest dreams that it could become a beautiful hotel again. But my mother, with no previous building or hotel experience, saw something different. She could see a beautiful boutique hotel and an amazing restored opera house. She even had enough vision to see a presidential suite on the top floor.

That hotel became Hotel Winneshiek, which is one of the nicest boutique hotels in the Midwest, with an amazing opera house to boot. And yes, the president, the secretary of state, and many movie stars, musicians, and dignitaries have stayed in the presidential suite. It has also helped revitalize what is now a vibrant downtown economy.

The power of vision!

SMALL TOWN, BIG DREAM

I was inspired enough by all this that I acquired a small, run-down coffee shop in the same town at the beginning of the Starbucks phenomenon. By the time I sold it, it was known as one of Iowa's best, and later was honored as the best coffee shop in all of Iowa. Take that, Starbucks!

I had never been in the coffee business, but I had researched and visited successful private coffeehouses around the country and had a vision of exactly what I wanted to do there. The shops I visited were not sterile, porcelain-tile, cold-looking stores, but were stores that made you feel you were in your living room. They were warm, with inviting colors, and you could picture yourself enjoying a great cup of coffee and a home-baked blueberry muffin. They were a little bit like the old TV show Cheers, in which everyone knew everyone else's name. I wanted a combination cof-feehouse and sandwich shop that would also be a gathering place for the community and make a positive impact on all involved.

You must begin with a vision, because it is a glimpse of pos-sibilities of a future. I have long emphasized this to young people. When I look at my archive of talks I've given at many youth orga-nizations and churches, I see that I was pushing that message as far back as the 1980s.

I would speak at least once a week on such topics to Souled Out youth movement gatherings, and I would challenge these young people to put what they learned to use. Without vision, as the Bible says, people perish, and the Bible is full of stories of visionaries who changed the world around them.

You have to look within yourself and see what inspires you. What are you thinking about all the time? What is your heart's desire? What sort of things would you be doing even without compensation? Who are the people who have had a major influence on you and who have encouraged you to give life to your ideas?

For me, the inspiration has been entrepreneurship itself, the excitement of starting something new. I know that I have the spirit of the pioneer, and that is what has driven my business initiatives. And I have a heart for helping young people. That is what sparked my devotion to the Souled Out youth movement. And it is why I am writing this book.

ASPIRING TO THE HEIGHTS

All my life I have seen people with vision accomplish great things. Bill Gates's vision of a PC in every house once seemed ridiculous, as did Steve Jobs's vision of a computer in every iPhone. But both Gates and Jobs made it to fame without a college degree. What they had was incredible vision, and they surrounded themselves with people who could help them turn that vision into something concrete. It wasn't as if they came from great wealth and built upon some existing empire. What they exhibited was grassroots ingenuity. They were pioneers who did not give up.

Starbucks founder Howard Shultz, sitting in an Italian café, noticed coffee bars on almost every block that served excellent espresso and also served as meeting places. They were a big part of Italy's society. That was the epiphany that inspired his vision of such a café in every neighborhood. Today, Starbucks has over 4,000 stores in 25 different countries, selling expensive and weird-sounding brews, and yes, the stores have become meeting places as well. It is part of our social landscape.

Walt Disney.

The story is widely told about the grand opening of Disney World's Epcot Center in Orlando, Florida. Walt Disney had recently passed away, so the Disney executives asked his wife to cut the ribbon and say a few words. When the master of ceremonies called her up to the podium, he smiled and said, "Mrs. Disney, I just wish Walt could have seen this!" She smiled and replied, "He did." The book *Walt Disney, an American Original* by Bob Thomas also chronicles Disney's vision of a cartoon mouse becoming a huge hit. The book relates how Walt would have a pilot fly him low over the thousands of acres of brackish swampland in central Florida as he sketched out his vision for Disney World.

Ray Kroc.

Ray Kroc, after opening his first McDonald's in Des Plaines, Illinois, said, "When I saw it working that day in 1954, I felt like some latter-day Newton who'd just had an Idaho potato caromed off his skull. That night in my motel room I did a lot of heavy thinking about what I'd seen during the day. Visions of McDonald's restaurants dotting crossroads all over the country paraded through my brain."

He extended his vision to every continent in the world, and today there are more than 35,000 McDonald's restaurants worldwide. Ray Kroc would often have breakfast at a local coffee shop while building his first location. The owner of the small, greasy-spoon diner would often chide him that no one was going to stand in line outside and order a 15-cent hamburger and 10-cent fries. That man and his restaurant are long gone while McDonald's restaurants took off like a rocket.

Do not be surprised when others, including your well-meaning friends, try to discourage you from pursuing your vision. In my early days of entrepreneurship I would often make a pilgrimage to Kroc's first restaurant in Des Plaines. It is still standing and is now a museum. Just sitting in the parking lot, I felt inspired to dream big dreams and think about the power of vision.

An interesting side note connects these two visionaries. During World War I, Ray Kroc met Walt Disney. According to Eric Schlosser, in his book *Fast Food Nation*, Kroc and Walt Disney happened to be ambulance drivers in the same Red Cross company. When Kroc first began selling McDonald's franchises around the country, he remembered Disney and sent him a letter in 1954. Disneyland was still under construction at the time, but Kroc sensed a great opportunity in having a presence at Disneyland. Kroc landed a deal with Disney, and McDonald's had a presence at Disneyland for many years. Great entrepreneurial minds have great vision.

Vision can be cultivated by identifying one's passion. We each have something powerful that motivates us. It may be a love of music, art, sports, or a love of entrepreneurship itself. Vision is essential for doing something grand. Vision is critical for business success.

As you aspire to your own heights, do your research. Who are the best in the field? Visit them. Find out as much as you can about them. In today's Internet-connected world it is easier than ever. When I was researching coffeehouses back in the mid-1990s, traveling around the country looking for what the best were doing to attract customers, the Internet hadn't gained much traction.

Today. anyone looking to learn about a business can do an online search and discover a gold mine of information. You can find lists and tips and bloggers aplenty who weigh in on their likes and dislikes.

Yes, it is easier than ever to get information online, as anyone who has ever called up a how-to video on YouTube can attest, but even though you can get much off the web, it is still best, whenever possible, to visit places to see, firsthand, the customer experience and how the business is run. We can't forsake the real world. The Internet has its downside. It is so easy to buy a book online, for example, but there's something to be said for going into a library and experiencing the architecture and the interactions and, maybe, actually meeting a librarian. If you are starting a business, you need to get out and talk to people one-on-one too. You need to see what is working or what is not working, and some of the best clues come from looking into the eyes of the customers and the staff.

PUTTING DREAMS IN WORDS

Vision can also be cultivated by speaking about it every chance you get. Talk to your wife or husband and other family members, to your friends and your associates. They will offer valuable suggestions, and people who know you well will likely have insights about your capabilities that you might not have recognized yourself.

Sure, you can "chat" with people online, and send out e-mails and texts, and technology does allow us to reach many people with high efficiency. By its nature, however, it is impersonal. It is not the same as sitting down for coffee with another human being who can see the enthusiasm on your face.

Something positive and creative happens as you verbalize your vision. It becomes clearer and clearer each time you speak about it. By distilling your idea into words for a receptive ear, you will be better able to think things through. When you need to explain your idea to someone, it helps to formulate exactly what you are proposing, how you would accomplish it, when and where you would start—the whole range of considerations. If something is missing or amiss in your thinking, a good listener will notice it right away and point it out to you. That is why, whenever I have launched into something new, I first have discussed the idea with just about anybody who will listen.

Also, write your vision down and reread it every day. Putting your ideas and your goals and dreams onto a sheet of paper, and then posting that sentence or that paragraph on the refrigerator, or wherever you will see it every day, has a powerful motivating effect. No longer is your idea just floating in the ether somewhere. It becomes far more than just something you muse about now and then. It becomes tangible, and that is what makes it seem all the more possible.

The best attitude is "all things are possible." Ariane van de Ven, a French trends consultant and strategist, recently spoke at a seminar I attended and said something that struck a chord with me: "Everything will be reinvented and people will reinvent the how, what, and why of every aspect of society."

In this day and age, nothing seems impossible. The technology of 3-D printing, smartphones, PCs, and DNA mapping points to an explosion of new ideas, inventions, breakthroughs, and vision. I believe that there is not one thing we use or experience daily that cannot be improved upon or reinvented. All it takes is keeping our eyes and ears open and constantly scouting the world for current needs and trends. Someone once said, "The fastest way to success is to find a need and fill it."

NEVER MIND THE NAYSAYERS

There will be many negative voices telling you, "You can't do this," or "Look at how many people fail." I heard such comments myself when we started our youth organization and put young people in leadership roles. "Oh, you are out of your mind," some said. "It just can't be done. You can't have these people leading worship groups. You can't have these kids leading trips around the world." But we did it. Despite all the flak at the beginning, people were amazed, once we got off the ground, at how much responsibility those young people could handle and what they could do.

When you encourage people and put faith in them, they can go miles farther than you might have imagined. In my machining business, I encourage that spirit of excellence to motivate everyone to do a better job and to put out a better product or to produce more. I have always hated the word *can't*. I know that with God, all things are possible.

When you look at the great inventors and entrepreneurs of the world, it seems they all faced negativity. I am sure that for each one who endured and prevailed, many others simply did not try, or gave up in the face of it, and what a loss for our society and culture. The Thomas Edisons and Alexander Graham Bells of our world—the examples through the centuries are countless—refused to take no for an answer and today we benefit from their dedication and persistence.

A clear vision and positive attitude will help you get past these minefields and accomplish your dreams as an entrepreneur. Vision will empower you when things get tough. Vision will energize each day and give you a reason to wake up in the morning. Vision is a very necessary ingredient to succeed in business.

As the Bible says, in Proverbs 29:18, "Where there is no vision, the people perish."

Big vision = Big results
Small vision = Small results
No vision = No results.

> "No man will make a great leader who wants to do it all himself or get all the credit for doing it."
>
> —ANDREW CARNEGIE
>
> *(who succeeded without a degree)*

....

CHAPTER 2

FLYING WITH EAGLES

E arly in my manufacturing career, as a CEO, I was invited to attend a bimonthly meeting with executives from six of my biggest competitors to discuss best practices and problems we mutually faced. These six companies were the eagles of our industry and larger than my company.

We would talk about everything from human resource (HR) concerns to the latest machines available to employee training and more. We would come to each meeting with some questions and issues on which we wanted advice, knowing that we could get all the help we needed by the time we left. I would receive welcome recommendations of suppliers of raw materials or finishing services we would need for our products, such as plating or heat-treating.

Every few months, we would take turns to meet in our respective factories and take a tour and have a great time. They would also share with me their wisdom and experience, as I was the youngest member. They inspired me for years to achieve more and grow. I am forever grateful.

I do not know how much they could have learned from me, although I am sure they appreciated the fresh spirit that I contributed, as the youngest member. Any group that hopes to gain a wide perspective needs people of diverse ages and backgrounds. Young people can take heart that the very people to whom they turn for advice will also, because of their wisdom, listen to them in return.

The opportunities of the Internet age have been quite lucrative for numerous young people, and I am not just talking about the Bill Gates types. I am talking about regular folks who have hit upon something that goes viral and suddenly they are wealthy. It can be stunning. But what matters more than the technology is the spirit. It is the belief that if you want to do something, there are ways. People found ways long before the Internet existed, long before the Industrial Revolution and assembly lines. It is all about ingenuity, and that is a quality young people should find in their elders, whether they embrace the latest electronics or not.

The good book says, "Iron sharpens iron, so one man sharpens another," and "Walk with the wise and become wise; associate with fools and get in trouble."

IN THE EAGLE'S NEST

In every business I have run, I have sought out the eagles, the brightest and the best, no matter where I had to travel or what the cost. You have to find the eagle's nest in order to find the eagles. The nest for you could be your trade association (join it), your chamber of commerce, the Rotary or Kiwanis or Lions Clubs, business growth seminars, management seminars, and so on. Networking with successful business people will work wonders for you, as an individual, and as the representative of a company. Do not isolate yourself. Seeking out the eagles will help to re-inspire you and reignite your business and vision.

The day I took over as CEO of our company, I joined our trade association, the Precision Machined Products Association (www.pmpa.com). Our previous CEO would have no part of it. He was afraid the competition would steal customers. This was not to be the case. You can't live in fear and isolate yourself from your competition. Joining our association, availing myself of its training and many resources, and networking with my fellow industry leaders was one of my best business decisions.

I have found that if you are humble, respectful, and resourceful, you can meet just about anyone you want to. The concept of "six degrees of separation" is that everyone is six or fewer steps away from any other person in the world; so a chain of "friend-of-a-friend" statements can be made to connect any two people in a maximum of six steps. In some situations, I believe this has shrunk to no more than three degrees of separation between you and just about any person you want to meet. For example:

- I wanted to meet the CEO of John Deere. I was at an awards dinner and noticed him sitting with other important business leaders at a table near the front. I asked around and found a friend who had met him once and asked him to introduce me. Two degrees of separation.

- I wanted to meet the director of one of the largest not-for-profit youth organizations in the country. I realized a good friend of mine knew him, so I asked for an introduction. No problem. Two degrees.

Sometimes, it is just that simple. I have been able to meet some of the best leaders in business and not-for-profit arenas simply by taking the time and making the effort to meet them while others are taking their coffee break or making idle chatter.

At any business seminar or conference, I will make it a point to meet the main speakers, introduce myself, and pick their brains. It is surprising how accommodating most people will be if you are kind and respectful. Be bold, focused, determined, and move out of the crowd.

There are also many online and social network opportunities including LinkedIn, Facebook, Twitter, Visible.me, and Plaxo, to name a few. They are valuable means of making contacts and managing one's online presence.

BENCHMARK AGAINST THE BEST

Every organization and industry has benchmarks—that is, they have standards of quality based on the experiences of others in the same industry. By paying close attention to those benchmarks, you can measure yourself against the best companies and the best practices in your field.

My youngest daughter got a job at Nordstrom, known for its legendary customer service. I was very excited—and why? I was happy for her, of course, but I was also pleased that when she started her job, they sent her home with a large training manual outlining their amazing customer service standards and practices. They told her to study it.

She not only studied it but I studied it as well. It was a gold mine to me because I could benchmark my customer service with theirs. Thank you, Nordstrom! My daughter shared many stories: If a customer needed something the next day that was not in stock, for example, she would personally drive to the nearest Nordstrom's store and have it ready for the customer the next day. Once, a customer, who was heading to the airport, left her bag in the store parking lot. Inside it were the sales receipt and her flight itinerary. A sales associate looked up her phone number, but nobody answered. Finally, the associate drove to the airport and had the customer paged and gave her the lost bag. Compare that with the subpar customer service you normally get at stores, and you will no doubt be impressed.

It does not matter what business you are in, customer service is customer service. In my precision machining business and in my consulting business, I continually benchmark against the best in the industry. Every chance I get to tour a bigger or better shop or learn more about my industry, I take. I want mine to be the best company, and I know which ones the best are so that I can measure myself against them in the hope that I will be able to surpass them.

No matter what kind of business you are in, whether it is retail, service, manufacturing, Internet, food, and so on, find the best companies and learn as much as you can about them—and I mean every little detail. Observe and ask questions, visit them, read about them, study them, and check out their websites. Do not be intimidated. Instead, be inspired. Set the bar high.

When I owned my coffee shop, I visited every great coffee shop that I could find, including, of course, the venerable Starbucks. I even bought Pour Your Heart into It, the book by founder Howard Schultz. I told my employees that they still could be successful even if a Starbucks were to open right down the street. (That did not happen, as this was a small college town.) But I wanted them to know what they had to offer to improve on the industry standard.

When I ran my youth organization, I visited and met with the leaders of some of the most successful youth organizations in the country. They were a tremendous help to me. Remember that you do not have to reinvent the wheel. People have spent much money and many hours and research efforts trying to solve problems you face today. The Internet is a gold mine of useful information, and when used with discretion, it can help you improve any area of your organization. Make the most of it.

In every business I walk into, I constantly observe best practices. I also take note of some of the worst practices. My wife has long been in the retail business, and she sometimes gets so offended by poor service from employees who seem to follow the worst practices that she has walked out of stores, sometimes leaving full shopping carts in her wake due to her frustration.

You can also learn a lot from your customers if you are willing to listen to them. Get past their reserve and your pride by asking for their opinions and advice on how you can improve on their customer experience.

How many times have you wanted to buy a product or service and had to wait an inordinate amount of time to pay, or get someone's attention, or stop being kept on hold on the phone? I am sure that you, like me, have had the experience of being put on hold for 20 minutes and reminded every 30 seconds by the recording that your call is "very important to us, so please hold." If my call is so important, how about hiring some extra staff to prove it?

We all experience some kind of poor customer service almost every day and we can readily give advice to those companies to improve their service. So why not develop a way to get customer feedback and use that information to improve your business?

One of the easiest ways to get feedback is to e-mail your customers a short customer service survey. Or you can hand out a postcard asking a few simple questions on which you would like to get some feedback. You need to also monitor social media results on sites such as Yelp, Google Reviews, and Facebook.

Usually, your customers will be pretty honest and give you good hints on what needs to be fixed or remedied. This is called social listening and it is becoming more and more vital. You must also take the time to monitor customer complaints. And last but not least, again, why not actually talk to your customers and solicit their comments? This seems basic, but few business actually practice that discipline.

Remember that you can always keep learning, from any business. Do not limit yourself to hobnobbing with other people in your own industry. Good ideas come from many directions. The auto industry, for example, has its own standards, but they also can be applied far and wide to other industries and businesses. You can learn much on a wide variety of topics, from sales to service to manufacturing.

Sound business principles are universal. Learn from the best! Apple, Nordstrom, Disney, Hilton, Toyota—read the books by their founders and other leaders, visit their headquarters, learn their best practices, and do not hesitate to apply them.

> "If you can't stand the heat,
> get out of the kitchen"
>
> —PRESIDENT HARRY S TRUMAN
>
> *(who succeeded without a degree)*

....

CHAPTER 3

THE BUCK STOPS HERE

When you enter my office, one of the first things you will see on my desk is this famous quote from President Harry S Truman: "The buck stops here." Another Truman quote is also a favorite of mine: "If you can't stand the heat, get out of the kitchen."

Both of these quotes remind me that I am the one who is ultimately responsible for the success or failure of my business. There is no one else to blame, no excuses, not the economy, the weather, the bank, the government, or the partners. Responsibility lies with me. Yet, in my experience, I have met too many business owners and ex-business owners and managers who seem full of these excuses.

Repeat after me out loud: "The buck stops here." That means that it stops with you, plain and simple. Now jump back on the horse, take the reins, and get the horse into overdrive. In other words, wake up! It is you and nobody else who is going to point the horse in the right direction as well as feed and water the rest of the herd.

You are the boss. Your employees have been patiently waiting for this moment. They want you to lead the way. They want you to wake up out of your carbohydrate-fueled stupor and be their boss. Period.

Believe me, it is easy to get stale, worn out, and burned out and just coast. I have had to have this wake-up call many times in my career. Recently, my two daughters joined me in the business and they could tell that I wasn't 100 percent there. In fact, in their direct yet sweet way, they let me know I had kind of checked out. Oh, I was there physically every day, but mentally, I was somewhere else. They needed me to be the boss again, and they helped to invigorate me so that I looked at the business with a fresh set of eyes.

Now, with that said, I will share with you another favorite quote, this one from Bill Cosby: "I do not know the key to success, but the key to failure is trying to please everybody."

As the boss, you have to make the hard decisions. That is why they pay you the dinero. You will never please everybody. Business is not a democracy. See how well that works in Washington. I am all for teamwork and team decisions, but in the end you still have to make the hard decisions. If you hope to succeed as a leader, you cannot be conflict averse, risk averse, or stubborn. You cannot be greedy, self-righteous, paranoid, or insecure. You must be a true leader. We've all heard that it is lonely at the top, and yes, that well can be the case way up there where the buck stops.

BEING A REAL BOSS

When I got into the coffee shop business, at first I did not show up a lot. Quite frankly, it was because the shop was over 300 miles away. When I did manage to show up, I handed out directives, gave advice, set goals, and walked out the door. But as soon as I left, the employees would go back to their own ways. They did not follow orders. I would visit weeks later to see that very little had changed or improved. I would give the same directions, and I would get the same results. In other words, there was no follow-through.

I have learned many times over the years that absentee ownership is a slippery slope. Most of the time, it does not work, especially in a new small business. I realized that I needed to put in a lot of time there to be successful. Once I did, there was a huge difference. My attitude changed, as did the attitude of the other people around me.

You can't assume that just because you are the owner, people will follow your orders as if you were a marine drill sergeant. They want you to be the boss, but you need to act like one before you will get the cooperation and performance that you desire.

Entrepreneurs sometimes think that businesses can run themselves. On the contrary, what is likely to happen is that they will run themselves out of business.

DEFINING RESPONSIBILITIES

Accountability is the obligation of an individual or organization to account for its activities, accept responsibility for them, and disclose the results in a transparent manner. It also includes the responsibility for money or other entrusted property.

In the spirit of "the buck stops here," you also must hold employees accountable as well as yourself. Their actions reflect on the entire company and its leadership.

In my manufacturing business the biggest cardinal sin is shutting down a customer's assembly line. Shutting down an auto or tractor assembly line causes lots of problems, costs lots of money, and creates a lot of ill will. Every employee in your customer's plant will hear about it, and your name will be mud.

In all my years, my business has never shut down a customer's line, though it has come very close a few times. That was due to a lack of communication with a secretary or a clerk that a shipment had to go out the door that night, no matter what the weather was like, or what the traffic problems or the dock closing times were. Some shipments have to be delivered by the 6 a.m. assembly line starting time, whether they are by truck, car, or air. You can't come in the next day and yell and scream about a missed shipment if you or your subordinates did not clearly communicate the absolute importance of on-time delivery.

If something goes wrong, or for that matter, if something goes right, who will be held responsible? You need to have clear descriptions of duty. It has often been said that if everyone is responsible, then no one is responsible. It happens in families. It happens in workplaces. It happens in national political leadership. If you do not define and delineate the roles clearly, you will make a mess of things.

You see this situation everywhere. It could be in any type of business, or in a church or a not-for-profit organization. People do well when they know what their responsibility is and when they know they are being held accountable. I think it is common in organizations for leaders to assume all the employees know what they are supposed to be doing, and it is not necessarily the case at all.

Assign responsibilities to specific employees and get them to verbalize to you that they know they are responsible and will be held accountable. Follow up with them.

I am not saying you should be patronizing, as in, "Now, repeat after me," or "Johnny, did you hear what I said? Let me hear you say it." Rather, each participant in a conversation should summarize it to make sure that the intent is clear and the message is understood. It is kind of like revisiting the talk you just had.

It is similar to what we do in sales: At the end of a sales call, we go over what we talked about so that both the salesperson and the customer are on the same page. A lot of times, a salesperson will discover that the customer heard something other than what was meant.

Similarly, a supervisor might discover that an employee did not get the point of the conversation. Hopefully, the boss will be reassured.

The talk might conclude like this: "All right, here's the project. So, Tom, as we discussed, you are going to be responsible for getting us this new supplier, and that will happen by next Monday."

"Right, that is exactly what we talked about. I'll be getting that supplier by Monday."

In effective writing and effective speaking you tell people what you will discuss, and then you discuss it, and then you tell them what you discussed. It is a principle of discourse because that is how people are best able to absorb information. We learn from reinforcement. That is good meat-and-potatoes advice.

I learned that, as a pastor. You reinforce the message week after week until people get to that "oh, yeah!" moment. Most pastors are up late Saturday night working on their message. When you write a sermon—and I have written hundreds of them—you have to understand human nature and how people come to grasp concepts. One is repetition, and churchgoers are familiar with the pastoral practice of asking the congregation to repeat a key phrase. Another way people grasp concepts is through storytelling. Jesus taught through the use of parables. He was communicating with people in a way he knew they would understand.

The application to entrepreneurship is critical. You need to make sure everyone understands exactly what is expected. In my years as an entrepreneur, I have been in many a meeting where important decisions were discussed ad nauseam until everyone agreed on the right answer and plan to go forward, and then everyone left, thinking that someone else was responsible for making it happen. This sounds ridiculous, but this scenario happens thousands of times a day in businesses all over the world. It is an epidemic of poor communication.

Employees must know clearly what they should be doing and when. Communicate, communicate, and then communicate some more. Communication is a major weakness in most businesses. Never assume. Employees deserve to get a clear statement of expectations. The boss can't legitimately get angry when employees fail to perform duties they never realized were theirs to do. "Well, it's obvious," the boss might think, but usually it is not.

Also, thorough training is important as a means of reflecting your expectations and vision for the company. I enjoy the television show *Undercover Boss*, in which the CEOs of large companies disguise themselves to work as undercover rank-and-file employees. So many times, the boss encounters employees who were poorly trained or who were never given the job expectations and standards that the corporate office assumed were being followed companywide. Watching the show gives you a great primer in business communication.

Every new employee should go through at least a weeklong training program that provides a healthy understanding of the company's history, its products, goals, vision, and core values.

They also need thorough training for the task to which they are assigned. Assign another employee to shadow new hires and be a mentor to them. If a new employee fails to perform adequately because duties weren't explained adequately, who is really the one at fault?

Do not follow my father's training program of "jump in the deep end and sink or swim!" My dad was such a naturally gifted, mechanically minded person that he just assumed everybody else thought as he did. He could look at anything mechanical and figure it out. He assumed his children and employees should be able to do likewise, and he threw us into jobs and situations that we knew nothing about and for which he did not give instruction.

A lot of companies make such assumptions about experience. The trouble with this sink-or-swim philosophy is that if you swim, that is great, but if you sink, you are dead in the water.

A GROWING AMBITION

At my company we train all our management in a system called the Rockefeller Habits, based on a book by that name written by Verne Harnish. We've been to some of his seminars, but we've had everybody work through that book quite a bit. It has been eye opening for our whole management team.

Second, because sales are the heartbeat of any business, we decided we needed to invest in all our salespeople, and so we got them into a top-level sales program that teaches the finer points of being a salesperson. That program has been operating for several months and we will continue it.

And third, we've started a program to train every single employee. I have 120 employees here. An educational company called Tooling University, part of the Society of Manufacturing Engineers, has an online school of over 400 interactive, and every single employee, including myself, has to go through the basic courses on manufacturing and machining.

Beyond that, they have to move on to other classes that are specific to their job, and our goal is that 5 percent of their paid time here each week will be used for training. So we have a training classroom set up with computers, and all of our employees are required to be retrained, whether they have been at our company for two weeks or for 45 years, which is how long one employee has been with us. Each of us is being retrained in the basics of quality, manufacturing, and safety.

We undertook this training program because we realized that if we weren't going forward, we were going backward. We saw that our competitors were moving full speed ahead, and we were determined to keep pace.

Many businesses felt the pain of the recent recession, and they have come through it knowing they must grow to survive. If you don't grow, someone else will take your place. We have a good company with a good product and good people, and that all points to growth. Companies have to stay competitive and relevant as times change. The key is to never stop learning.

And so it is a three-prong approach that we are using to grow the business, and it involves, basically, retraining everybody from the top down. I, personally, have gone to all three of the programs: the management, the sales, and the Tooling University programs.

I know that I too can continually improve and learn new things, and, as the CEO and leader, I need to know what everybody else is learning too.

The sales program, for example, is counterintuitive to what I have learned in the past. It differs from what you would think a salesperson would need to do, or say, or be. Salespeople tend to be hungry to get an order from a customer. They go in, give their spiel, and do all the talking about why their product or company is best. However, our sales program teaches us to keep our mouths shut. If a salesperson talks, the customer is not talking. And if the customer's not talking, the salesperson is not going to get the sale.

We must listen rather than talk, and ask questions, and try to find our customers' "pain"—that is, are they experiencing a problem, and what's causing it? That is where you'll make the sale. Sales do not come from writing quote after quote. They come from understanding why the customer wants the quote to begin with. I understand the feeling. Salespeople have called on me to try to interest me in a new machine. I'll sit for a presentation, and all the salespeople do is give me a speech. They do not even find out whether I need that particular machine. They'll walk out of the office thinking I am interested, but I have just been bored for a half hour.

In a way, the lesson there reminds me of what kids with a job at McDonald's should do. Rather than assuming they know it all, they should keep their mouth shut, listen, observe, and ask a whole lot of questions. That is how you learn things. If that system works in sales, it will work in developing a career.

Our 5 percent dedication to training is the standard among world-class companies and it applies even to our lowest-paid, $10-an-hour workers. Some people might argue that this training throws away 50 cents an hour of productivity for each of them. I do not see it that way. The benefits are better production, higher-quality work, fewer mistakes, and less frustration. We have found that people are a lot more motivated in their jobs when they learn the latest, cutting-edge practices. Some of our seasoned engineers who have been around the block quite a few times are taking these classes and learning new methods.

We tell people, "Readers are leaders and leaders are readers." Equipped with better knowledge, an employee can take on more responsibility in a higher-level job at greater pay so both the company and the employee gain. Training programs are a good way to identify executive talent, and that is why they include leadership and communication classes. You can also identify the whiners and complainers who aren't likely to do much except hold your company back.

Most employees will appreciate their company's efforts to help them improve. "They know that I exist," the workers will think, "and they are showing they care about me." Many of my 120 employees speak Spanish and so, when we rolled out our program, we offered it in their language as well. They were excited to have this opportunity.

An informed and grateful employee can become a productive, loyal, and valuable employee. Invest the time and effort needed because the dividends are great.

ACCOUNTABLE TO THE ACCOUNTING

In a chapter titled "The Buck Stops Here," it is only fitting that we talk about accounting. With accounting, you either love it or lose it. You either embrace the importance of accounting, or you stand to lose a lot of money.

One of the biggest failures that you see in business is that people do not understand accounting. They do not know what their profit margins are. They do not know what their true costs and expenses are or what their break-even sales level is. They go at it blindly. Often, they let someone else do it with little oversight. Many do not even know how to read a financial statement. It is very important that you know how to read your financial statement. Ask your accountant, search on the web, take a junior college course on finances, ask a business friend, but whatever it takes, understand the basics of your statement. Swallow your pride and ask.

I learned early in my career the importance of good accounting and timely reports. When I started my rent-a-car business, I was getting reports from my accountant as late as one and two months after the fact. I'd be in the dark. If we lost money in January, I wouldn't know about it until March. I learned the hard way that I have got to be on top of the accounting. It is essential that I know what numbers are important and whether I am making any money.

It is a shame that a lot of small business entrepreneurs actually do not know if they are making money or not. Then, two years later, they find themselves $100,000 in debt or in some big hole they can't get out. It is startling that they cannot give a clear answer on that. They might guess they will be all right, but a guess is not good enough.

It is amazing how many businesses run that way. They lack the necessary systems. That is the beauty of buying a franchise in which all those systems are set up for you. You can just walk into it without the uncertainties that so many start-ups face. You still have to work hard, but at least you are getting good information. You are still the boss, and you are still responsible for whether the business thrives or dies, but your odds of making it increase substantially because of the built-in expertise.

People do not think of themselves as accountants. Many people hate dealing with numbers. It is just not who they are. But who you are is not what the business is. The business needs someone who is giving the accounts serious oversight. Whether you know numbers or not, you've got to make them your business.

Most entrepreneurs I have run across are definitely visionaries and emotionally attached to their business. That blinds them to the realities of accounting and good accounting. They often have a blind faith that they have a great business, a great product, and they are going to make it. The reality is that banks look at it differently, and so do accountants. Passion is important to business success, but passion alone won't balance the books.

Many years ago one of my cousins and her husband had a successful baking company. Her best friend was their accountant. But the problem was the friend had fallen into some serious personal financial problems and, after a few years, was convicted of embezzling tens of thousands of dollars. The money was never recovered.

It was discovered when my cousin came back from a vacation and another employee informed her that her bookkeeper had put in very few hours that week and yet had paid herself for a full week's work. With that information, my cousin suspected the possibility of fraud in other areas. For some reason, every month, they were always struggling with cash flow.

She went to the bank to personally see copies of all the checks that had been written. To her dismay, she discovered her bookkeeper had cashed, with a forged signature, checks worth at least $60,000 over a six-month period. The bookkeeper would always meet the mail, be the first to get the bank statement, and then reconcile the account before my cousin and her husband saw it.

Once this was discovered, the police were called and the woman was promptly arrested. She was sentenced to two years in prison and ordered to make restitution. She served one and a half years, was released early, and then disappeared. No restitution. My cousin had used an outside accountant to reconcile the books every month. He had not caught the fraud, so he was promptly fired.

My cousin learned the hard way the importance of keeping a keen eye on the accounts, no matter how busy you are or how trustworthy you think the accountant is. It is a sad tale repeated over and over among entrepreneurs. They put someone in charge and money goes missing for a number of reasons including gambling or drug problems, family debt, or hard times.

I have a friend who operated an auto business. He put his best friend in charge of handling the accounts. The business was successful and going well until he discovered his friend had a gambling problem at the racetrack and was gambling away the sales tax money that he had said was being sent regularly to the state. Much money was owed, and my friend eventually had to close the business. I have heard these same stories many times over the years. They are very common tales in new businesses and even in well-established businesses.

Lesson: Be on your guard. You cannot assume all is well, even if you have a controller. The people in charge of the accounts must know you are looking over their shoulder.

In other words, keep your accountant accountable, because, in the end, the buck, once again, stops with the owner. If you want to learn more about this, I have included an appendix that lists the top 10 internal controls to prevent and detect fraud. Among them is a system of checks and balances to ensure no one person has control over all parts of a financial transaction. You also need to protect petty cash and other cash funds, learn how to protect checks against fraud, restrict the use of company credit cards, reconcile bank accounts, and so on.

CASH FLOW IS KING

It is very important to know about money matters in general. It is not enough for businesspeople to see plenty of customers or clients coming through the door and figure everything must be working out all right. They may know they are busy, but do they have a handle on their cash flow or their margin? You can be operating a successful and profitable business, but if you do not control your cash flow, you can find yourself going out of business.

In simple terms, if your accounts receivable (money that people owe you) are out at 90 days, and your accounts payable (money that you owe to your suppliers) are out at 30 days, it won't take long before you run out of money. But you have all these orders, you say. Even if you have a good line of credit at your local bank, you still will eventually run out of money. Why? Because in every business, you hit slow times, seasons, or recessions.

That is why it is so important to know and look at your numbers. You can't accept an accounting system that reports numbers back to you two weeks after your month-end close because by then it will be too late to correct something that could have saved you a lot of money. You need to watch your numbers daily and weekly. There are many accounting and payroll software packages available, along with tutorials to walk you through them. QuickBooks is a good place to start your search; you can go online and get a free trial.

There is no excuse for financial ignorance. Prior to the recent recession, we noticed at our company that the banks were getting a little skittish and we sensed that things were slowing down. The numbers were not trending right, and our bank saw it. Numbers do not lie, so we took steps to cut back expenses and through early, decisive action, we weathered the economic downturn while a lot of our competitors did not.

Important note: Your banker can be your best friend or your worst enemy. Take the time to foster a good relationship with your bank and also have a back-up bank in case your present relationship deteriorates. Know your bottom line, and know your break-even numbers. Get rid of all unnecessary expenses and be merciless about avoiding purchases that cannot positively affect your bottom-line profits. You are in business to make a profit, and there is nothing wrong with that.

If you are starting a new business, you should have a year's worth of cash squirreled away for the business to survive through a worst-case scenario. Too many excited and wishful entrepreneurs launch their businesses with no capital to fall back on, thinking erroneously that they will be an overnight success. They invest all their money up front and then realize that they have little to fall back on during those lean start-up months. I recently read an article in *Crain's Chicago Business* about three fairly new retail businesses in Chicago that failed when the recent Chicago winter (one of the three worst in its history) caused pipes to burst in the streets and utility bills to soar, and also kept customers away for a month and a half while they cozied up in their homes rather than shopping in miserable below-zero weather. Not having an adequate financial cushion is a major reason that 80 percent of new businesses fail within the first 18 months.

A man I knew was determined to open a cupcake shop even though, for months, everyone told him to wait until he had more of a cash reserve. He was too emotionally connected to the project, as many new entrepreneurs are, and he wouldn't listen to any practical wisdom. The business began with no reserves. The end of the story was not pretty and the stress it caused him and his family was tremendous. It could have been avoided.

For ongoing businesses, there are many potholes on the road to success. Many of them are unpredictable; for example, the loss of a key customer, or new competition, or a recession. This is why it is so important to have cash reserves available, just in case. Cash flow is king.

FIVE RULES FOR SUCCESS

As we close this chapter, I want to emphasize five important rules for your success:

1. You are the one who is ultimately responsible for the success or failure of your business.

2. Your employees want and need you to be the boss and leader, so act like it. You always can become a better boss than you are now, so learn and keep on growing.

3. You must give clear responsibilities to your employees and hold them accountable for accomplishing them.

4. Good communication is an essential element of success. Never assume an employee will understand right away what is expected, particularly if you have not made it clear.

5. Know your finances and accounting. Know your profit margins, and keep your expenses and your purchases as low as possible. Ignorance may be bliss, but ignoring these rules will sink your business.

> "You are only as good as
> the people you hire."
>
> —RAY KROC
>
> *(who succeeded without a degree)*

....

CHAPTER 4

HIRE SLOWLY, FIRE QUICKLY

Business is a lot like baseball. You are hiring a team: employees, managers, marketers, front office staff, and everyone you need to win the game. Some people are pitchers, some are catchers, some are first basemen, some are shortstops, and some are way out in left field.

In baseball, it is usually the whole team that contributes to winning or losing. This includes the managers, coaches, star players, and rookies. Business owners operate much like a ball team's general manager. They want the best players available, and they also want some rookies they can coach and train to do the job with skill and expertise. I try to think like a coach when hiring. I have to not only develop my employees just as a coach does, but also put them in the right positions.

To win in your business, you want to hire as many star team players as your budget can afford. That means that you need to hire smart and not just fill positions. You may have to go through hundreds of applications to find the right one or two people who would be excellent for your company. It is not easy, but the time and effort you spend will be worth it.

The movie *Moneyball* is a great primer on hiring and firing. Watch it, and then watch it again. General manager Billy Beane is a master of putting the right players in the right positions. Under his watch, the Oakland A's have become the most cost-effective team in baseball, making the play-offs far more often than any of my Chicago teams!

In 2009, *Sports Illustrated* named Beane as the 10th top GM/executive of the decade in all of sports. He knows how to hire and fire, and that will be the greatest challenge for those who aspire to be business owners.

Beane was excellent at finding people to strengthen his weaknesses and do it within a budget. In business, we all have a budget. We can't just go out and hire all superstars. You hire a few superstars, and then the rest you just hire for skills that show potential.

In running a business, the more time you can put into the hiring process, the better. You realize it is a team effort, and every person on that team is important and plays a role.

Employees are usually a huge cost for your business and they can make or break your business. You must learn how to interview prospective hires and I would suggest you have other team members involved in the process. You may want to have a second interview involving a manager or a department head and, of course, your HR person if you have one.

I have included in the appendices a list of the 20 most important common interview questions. It is important that you familiarize yourself with these and not be shy about asking many questions before hiring people. Make sure you check out their references, especially for top positions.

Early in my career, I hired a full-time consultant for one of my organizations. He was great as a consultant, and so I figured he would be a good prospect for hiring as a full-time employee. He looked and talked and acted like a superstar hire.

Warning sign! The adage that "if it looks too good to be true, it is" applies here. I did not do my homework and never bothered to call his former employers. I thought I had a good relationship with him and his excellent track record, as a consultant, would guarantee he would be a good full-time hire.

A year later and $100,000 poorer, I fired him, and it was only then that I made the phone calls. I called his former boss on the West Coast and found that this person had a record of costly bad habits and ideas that had almost driven his former employers out of business. One former boss even broke into tears when he told me that he wished I had called him first before hiring this person full-time. I wish I had too!

I am going to give you some principles on hiring that will save you a lot of heartache and headaches.

DOWN WITH TOM, UP WITH SUZY

The number-one mistake that managers make is to hire solely on the basis of expertise, without considering prospects' attitudes and willingness to grow as functioning team players. For many years in business, I put up with employees who were good at what they did but who had bad attitudes. I felt they were indispensable and I could overlook a poor attitude. Wrong! I finally realized that a bad attitude is deadly poison for a team and for a business.

A young man named Tom once walked into my office with the skills for the position that I was looking to fill. He had been unemployed for over a year and had a small family to support. I offered him a fair starting wage and an opportunity for quick advancement. His response startled me. He said, "Sir, I can make more money than that just by sitting at home collecting food stamps and government assistance." He turned down the job.

I realized that, with his attitude, he would never be a success in life, and I was grateful that I had not hired him. He would have served only as an example to my employees of how to be lazy and unproductive. I have, for many years, systematically let people go for a bad attitude. If you have one, you will not work for me. Period.

And then there was Suzy. I once owned and ran one of the first used-car rental agencies in Chicago, which I called—and I kid you not—Dirt Cheap Rent-a-Heap. Business was very good, but it also was hectic. We would rent old cars and vans to people for half of what they might pay at Hertz or Avis. We were swamped.

In walks this full-of-life college girl named Suzy, asking for a job. After a brief interview, we hired her, and from day one, she became our superstar. She would do everything from running the counter, prepping cars, accounting, customer service, parts ordering, and whatever else the business needed. She could do the job of three people and had a great attitude to boot.

So the objective, by whatever means, is to try your best to hire top talent. Go for the gold. There are a lot of Suzies out there.

RULES FOR HIRING

Here, then, are my rules for hiring and retaining good employees:

1. Do not accept any bad attitudes. A bad attitude spreads like the flu, and if you do not stop it, it will make your whole team sick. Good attitudes will spread too, so look to hire people with a positive nature. Is the prospective hire full of complaints about previous employers? Do not be surprised if you become the next target of such whining. No one is indispensable. I have interviewed people who clearly were bright and skilled, and yet, afterward, I felt like telling them not to let the door hit them on the way out. I have never regretted my decision to insist on good attitudes.

2. Hire friends very cautiously. They can become your best employees, but often, they are your worst, and they are hard to fire. Hire family members even more cautiously. Let them know the ground rules and expectations up front. And treat them like the rest of

your employees. I hear horror stories all the time from business people who are suffering because of family involvement. But it also can work very well. I can attest to having two of my brothers working very well with me for over 20 years, and recently, two daughters and two sons-in-law.

3. **Hire not only for skills but also for potential.** Leaders can be made if trained and motivated properly. I have seen many a young person with no previous experience or knowledge of my business learn a trade or skill and prosper and excel. Many times, it is even an advantage to start from the beginning with someone who does not have the baggage of bad habits or practices from a previous employer.

4. **Put people in the right positions.** Test them for their personality and skill sets. There are many tests, such as Meyers Briggs and the DISC profile. It is hard, sometimes, to understand where people fit, which is why we try to use testing to learn about their particular skills.

5. **Hire great employees who can strengthen your weaknesses.** It is very important to know your own skill set. You cannot do everything yourself. You may need to learn about all aspects of the business, but you will soon see the areas that do not come naturally to you. Do not try to be a superstar, because you will be at risk of burning out. Instead, hire smart. Bring people aboard who will bolster your weak areas.

6.   If all else fails, temporary services can work in a number of ways. They are a way to fill an immediate need. They also help with your cash flow and can act as a filter to find qualified people whom you can hire full-time in the future. If the employee does not work out, call the temporary agency for someone else. I have been amazed at how many good employees we have found over the years through temporary labor agencies.

7.   Reward only your great employees. Let them know they are appreciated and that they are an integral part of making your team successful. Monetary rewards are great, but they are not always the answer. An encouraging word and a pat on the back are good for everyone involved and are sorely lacking in most companies. Also, when your less-than-great employees see this, they will either wise up and change or seek another job.

8.   Fire quickly. You will know if there is a bad apple. A rotten apple will never become a tasty one. You should be able to see right away when people are not pulling their weight and are bringing the rest of the team down. You must fire quickly to end your suffering and your team's suffering.

NO ROOM FOR NEGATIVITY

Hiring and firing are two of the most important things you will do in your business. They are also two of the hardest and most challenging things you will do.

As a small business owner, you will find this to be much more important and strategic than what your large-corporation counterpart deals with. When you have only a few employees, each one is vitally important to your company, whereas in a large corporation, losing one or two employees does not make a big difference.

You have to become good at hiring and firing. Your ability to do so is what will make or break your company. Most people who get to the point where they are interviewing prospective employees have experienced, over the years, how refreshing it is to be surrounded by positivity, and they have felt the drain of negativity. The place to make the difference is at the starting gate. That is always important with any hire, but it is particularly the case when hiring and training salespeople. They are the ones who keep business coming through your door.

Over a 40-year period, I have had to fire a considerable number of employees. I have never enjoyed it, and I have never taken it lightly. But at the same time, I have had very few regrets concerning firings, and when I have felt such regret, it was because I had not dealt with the matter much sooner.

Early in my life, I was surrounded by many negative people. I finally realized that I had a choice and decided that I had no time for them. This is not only a rule but also a strong boundary in my life. I choose not to participate in or allow negative speaking or attitudes.

Call me an optimist, but to me, life is way too short to put up with people who seem determined to drag down those around them. I have benefitted from applying a truth that was written nearly three millennia ago and that still rings true today. It is found in the book of Proverbs, chapter 18, verse 21: "Death and life are in the power of the tongue; and they that love it shall eat the fruit thereof."

"He who does not economize
will have to agonize."

—CONFUCIUS

(who succeeded without a degree)

....

CHAPTER 5

NEVER PAY RETAIL

In the precision manufacturing company where I am the CEO, we use very sophisticated machines and very expensive ones. They can cost anywhere from $100,000 to $1.5 million.

But every month, across the country, there are three to five manufacturing plants with similar equipment that is going to auction. It happens for many reasons: retirement, corporate takeover, illness of an owner, the economy, bad business decisions, downsizing, or going out of business for whatever reason.

This means that there are many opportunities to buy pre-owned equipment in good condition. Many times, I have been able to buy a great CNC (computerized numerical control) machine only a few years old. We bought one machine, which retails new for $1.5 million, for a third of that price, when a new manufacturing plant went bankrupt. The machine was rarely used and only two years old.

This machine was a 16-station, CNC, turning machine, which most automotive companies use to produce millions of precision mechanical components for their vehicles. Imagine an amazing machine that simultaneously drills, turns, mills, and threads 16 parts at a time.

You can find these auctions at www.bidspotter.com as well as other auctions sites that list equipment for a wide variety of businesses. But buyer beware. You must do your homework and research the items as thoroughly as possible, and if possible, you should pay a visit to physically inspect what you intend to purchase. Even so, you run a risk. The best of the best machinery buyers sometimes get burned, but the risk does not outweigh the benefits.

Remember, there are many businesses that go under within two years. Restaurants, for example, often do not last more than a year, and that means barely used equipment is sold for a song at some of these auctions. I have seen kitchen equipment sell for pennies on the dollar. So why would you buy new equipment? Use the savings to advertise and grow your business.

If you need office furniture, you can get it even cheaper at auctions. Usually, at the end of many auctions, after all the plant items are sold at the end of a long day, the auction staff will practically give away the office equipment if you move it out. I have seen whole corporate offices that included desks, chairs, credenzas, bookshelves, and more go for little more than pennies.

I was at a corporate headquarters in Chicago that had a beautiful lecture hall complete with state-of-the-art audio equipment, video screens, soundboards, speakers, and other equipment, as well as all the tables and chairs. It resembled a college lecture hall. The sound system alone would have cost well over $100,000 to install new, but the whole package went for $4,000. Amazing.

I was at another corporate auction that had a beautiful cafeteria and a fully equipped professional-grade kitchen. It was a manufacturing plant, so most of the buyers were there to buy machines, not kitchen equipment. They had ice makers, restaurant-grade stoves and refrigerators, mixing equipment, and more. It all was auctioned off very late in the day, when there were few people left to bid. The equipment went for pennies on the dollar. I only wished I had a restaurant at the time that could have used all that equipment.

FRUGALITY PAYS

As my second-generation-American father would have done, you have to pinch pennies to make money. Being frugal in a world that tempts us to buy more and more is a challenge. From birth, we are barraged with thousands of commercials and messages that have programmed our minds to think that we need to buy, buy, buy, and that we must have the latest invention or product that comes along. We have become a people who can't stand to keep an expensive cellphone or tablet for more than a year. Or we think the newest car will make us a more important person or we need another credit card to enjoy life to its fullest.

Most entrepreneurs follow suit. They spend big and have big expectations, falsely thinking that in no time, they will be able to pay off the big expenditures they are making. They do all this without taking the time needed to build that business. So if you want to help cut some of those costs, you should really do your research and buy smart.

To the savvy businessman, there is much money to be saved. Good deals abound, as on eBay and Craigslist, to name a few outlets. They provide you with great ways to save on normal business items. So do your homework!

After my father passed away in 1991, and my brothers and I pored over all the financial records from the years before, we found that he had been very careful with his money. He saved a lot on the little things, making do with what he had, before he would spend large sums of money. In fact, his main rule was to pay for everything up front and not finance it. If he did not have the money in the bank, he wouldn't buy it. Because of his frugality, he was able to make an excellent living for himself and his family.

Being frugal is wise, and there are many ways to begin. Why not use Priceline—where you name your own price—when looking for a hotel? Why should you travel first-class or business everywhere you go? The lesson from the greatest generation, which endured the Great Depression, was to be careful with a dollar, and that is a lesson that is even more pertinent in today's changing and global economy.

THE WISE STEWARD

I am not cheap. I am just trying to be a wise steward of money. I appreciate how hard it is to make a buck.

As a buyer, you are in control. You have the money in your hand. The seller is at your mercy. Always ask for a discount. If you do not, you will never get one. The seller is not likely to say anything worse than one little word, "No." And often, you will hear "Yes." You will be surprised at what you can get if you just ask, especially if you do so in a kind and respectful way.

If your budget is limited or you are starting out on a shoe-string, it is critically important to be frugal. Even the late Sam Walton of Wal-Mart fame, who was one of the richest men in the world, would drive to his stores in an old pickup truck.

Many business people, believe it or not, never think of searching for alternatives. They pay retail prices unnecessarily and waste thousands of dollars. All those failing start-up companies are putting a lot of like-new equipment on the market, so you have a wide assortment of choices.

TWELVE RULES OF NEGOTIATION

Everything can be negotiated. A study from the Market Watch Center for Negotiations found that "negotiators typically lose up to 42 percent of the total potential value of a transaction." That is a lot of money left on the table that you could use in your business. There are many great books on negotiation. Take the time to study them, and you will not regret it.

Before any negotiation, the first and most important command is this: Research, research, research, and do it ahead of time. Only then will you be ready to dip your foot into the pool of negotiations.

HERE ARE MY 12 RULES OF NEGOTIATION:

1. **Have the price you want to pay solidly in your mind.** Do not get caught up in the moment. Most minds do not do well when they are under pressure. Emotions will get in the way of sound judgment.

2. **Never make the first offer.** If you do, you will leave money on the table. If you make the make the first offer, you establish the range of the negotiation. Instead, wait until you get a figure, and then make your counteroffer.

3. **Let the seller speak first.** Your silence is an effective tool. You do not want to unwittingly give the seller any clues as to how much you might be willing to spend.

4. **Remember that, as the buyer, you have the money, so you are in control.** If you do not agree to the sale, there will be no sale, and that is a position of power.

5. **Everyone likes cash, so pay in cash if you can.** Cash speaks louder than credit.

6. **Practice your poker face.** Do not appear to be excited. Your enthusiasm will tip off the seller that you might be willing to pay more. Again, the less you speak, the better.

7. **Be ready and willing to walk away.** There will be other deals. If this one does not meet the figure you have in mind going in, you should not be tempted to go beyond your boundaries.

8. **If a deal seems too good to be true, it really usually is.** The red lights should be flashing on this one. Pay attention to your instincts.

9. **Let the seller do most of the talking.** Listen for his motivation and hunger to sell. If you detect that the seller badly needs this deal, you may have more room to negotiate a lower price.

10. **Do not be afraid of making a low-ball offer.** The seller can only say no, but many times, will say yes. Sometimes the seller just wants to move things along so he can get back to business.

11. **Let the seller know you are looking at alternatives, and that you have done your research.** The seller will respect you when you make it clear that you know what you are talking about, and that you understand what the market will bear.

12. Be personable and keep things light hearted. Being rude or obnoxious gets you nowhere. You may think that you are being "tough," but such a stance could backfire on you and cause you to lose the deal.

Following those 12 rules consistently will help you to economize. It takes a lot of money to run a business and there are always unexpected expenses that will come up. So it is wise to save and be frugal in every area of your business. Make it a practice to follow these rules daily, starting now, not someday in the future. Be frugal and make money!

"My success, part of it certainly, is that I have focused in on a few things"

—BILL GATES

(who succeeded without a degree)

CHAPTER 6

....

THE POWER OF THE CHECKLIST

Many years ago, an efficiency expert visited Charles Schwab, president of an obscure steel company. In trying to encourage the company to use his services, the efficiency expert presented several methods of management.

"We already know too much," Schwab finally told him. "What we need is something to help us do what we already know we should be doing. Show me how to get more things done with my time, and I will pay you anything you ask, within reason."

The efficiency expert, Ivy Lee, told Schwab that in 20 minutes he could show him something that could make him 50 percent more efficient. Then he handed Schwab a sheet of paper and told him to write down the six most important things he had to do the next day and number them according to their priority.

The heading, "In the Morning," instructed Lee to take the top priority item and work on it until done. Then, through the day, he was to go on to numbers two and three in the same manner. He was advised not to worry if he did not finish all six items because, after all, he would have focused on the most important things anyway.

"Do this every working day and get your employees to do the same," Lee told Schwab. "After trying it for as long as you like, send me a check for what you think the idea is worth."

A few weeks later Schwab sent Lee a check for $25,000 with a note saying the priority list was one of the most important lessons he had ever learned. As Charles Schwab applied the plan over the next five years, Bethlehem Steel grew from an unknown company to one of the largest independent steel producers in the world. Schwab, needless to say, became a millionaire.

Years later, Schwab's friends, upon hearing this story, asked him if he did not think $25,000 was a rather high fee for such a simple idea. Schwab replied that in its simplicity lay its greatness, and it was, perhaps, the single best investment he ever had made.

A businessperson must use a priority checklist, not just a to-do list. Schwab realized that with his busy schedule and multiple responsibilities, he needed a way to keep his priorities in order, and the priority list was his answer.

Most successful people take care of the most important things first while most unsuccessful people save the most important things until last. Nonessential trivia and busyness will waste the day and prove very unproductive.

A STRATEGY IN YOUR POCKET

The priority checklist will help you to utilize one of the greatest time-saving devices in the world: the little two-letter word no. The list enables you to say no to the many things that have nothing to do with your most important business objectives and that can so easily distract you from the important matters at hand.

A checklist helps you to keep your focus. For example, the Internet, as valuable as it is for finding resources, can also become an insidious waste of your time. A lot of people, if they are not focused, will go on the web and sit for hours looking at interesting tidbits and perusing the latest trivial news. It is so easy to let the currents pull them out to sea. Meanwhile, they are not attending to their job duties. They may think it will take just a moment to pay a bill or check out Facebook, but how often does that moment turn into many minutes? It sucks away precious time, and anyone who manages a business should be concerned about that loss of productivity. That is a big problem in business today, as studies have shown.

A checklist can help you say no to other distractions such as all those nonessential phone interruptions. You do not have to take every phone call. We all get calls that we should put off for another time. And it is so easy to fill up time with matters of the moment that are far from being priorities. A checklist will help you to organize what's most important for the day, or for the week. You are less likely to pursue the trivial or to daydream when you have a clear list of what needs to be accomplished.

It requires foresight to create a checklist. You are forcing yourself to think things through. We all have so many things going on in our personal and family lives. We have issues with our friends and our children and our finances. But when you are on the job, all that needs to be set aside. You need to focus on why you are there. With a checklist in your pocket, you can push those distractions to the side for the moment. You can put them on a shelf to deal with later.

I have been using a pocket checklist for the last 25 years. I start the day with a blank 3-by-5 note card, and I list on it the top five or ten things that I want to get done that day. I then put it in my shirt pocket and refer to it a few times during the day. At the end of the day, I am always amazed at how many things I have managed to cross off the list.

This little tool will help you get a minimum of 20 percent more accomplished. I am a firm believer. Next time you see me, ask to see the card; it is always with me. You may not get all of the items on your list done, but you will accomplish a lot more than if you did not have it at all. I have had many people try the pocket checklist, and they often have told me they get 50 percent more accomplished. Go ahead. Give it a try.

A MUST FOR BUSINESSES TODAY

Checklists have become a must in many businesses these days. I was talking to a good friend who works for a school bus company, and he related to me that before he drives the bus out of the yard each day, he has to go through a checklist of 105 items. It includes such details as checking the oil, the tire pressure, the outside condition of the bus, the mirrors, and more.

Another friend who is an airline pilot told me that he had a checklist of 400 items that had to be completed before he was permitted to take off down the runway. Hospitals and surgeons now use checklists before and after they perform surgeries. These checklists have saved thousands of lives since they were introduced years ago.

Every business can benefit from a checklist. McDonald's famously uses checklists to ensure uniformity and quality of products and service so that you get the same experience in any country. I personally can vouch for that, even when traveling overseas.

A checklist can improve quality in any area. Think of it as a recipe. In my coffeehouse, I had a personal recipe for what I feel is the best gingersnap cookie on the planet, but you have to follow the steps in the order written in the recipe. I would give this recipe to my cooks, they would make it, and then I would sample a cookie.

Immediately, I could tell if the recipe was not followed exactly. The cookies would be hard, and the taste different. I would ask my cooks if they had followed the recipe (checklist) completely.

They would all say yes. Then, I would pull out the recipe and go over it line by line, ingredient by ingredient. Sure enough, every time, we would find that an ingredient had been left out, or substituted with something similar but not what was specified, or the oven temperature had been adjusted in error. It seemed that if the recipe was not followed 100 percent, we would not get the best gingersnap on the planet.

SAFEGUARD AGAINST HUMAN ERROR

The beauty of the checklist is that it can prevent human error if it is properly followed. Can you imagine what would happen to my pilot friend if he had to remember all 400 items without a written checklist, or if he used the checklist and decided that he did not want to check off all the items? Humans are not 100 percent accurate in their recall and performance, so we need to check and recheck.

Think of tasks and procedures in your business that you constantly have to remind your employees to do. You can develop a simple checklist that your employees can sign to indicate they followed your instructions on the list. Remember to keep it simple and efficient.

Complexity will kill a checklist. Human nature is easily overwhelmed when faced with too many complicated instructions. Long lists can be divided into a number of shorter lists so they can be more easily grasped and understood. Take it in small bites. And the simpler the language, the better.

Scott Jacobson, president of Sightline Business Advisors, wrote a white paper titled "Use This Checklist or People Die." In it he provides the following checklist for creating a checklist:

1. Target areas that are underperforming.

2. Establish a benchmark for improvement.

3. Document the sequence of tasks for each person involved.

4. Prioritize each task and identify those that are essential.

5. Identify every area where a decision is made or judgment is required

6. Implement a checklist and measure results.

7. Create a checklist for future edits. Do not assume you will get it right the first time.

The power of the checklist is a beautiful thing. It is a tool that every successful business must use. For more on this subject, I recommend the book *The Checklist Manifesto* by Atul Gawande. This is an excellent study of checklists and it will help you see how to apply checklists to every area of your business and save yourself a lot of time, effort, and stress.

> "A goal is a dream with a deadline."
> —NAPOLEON HILL
> *(who succeeded without a degree)*

....

CHAPTER 7

THE POWER OF DEADLINES

n May 25, 1961, President John F. Kennedy announced before Congress and the American people the ambitious goal of sending an American safely to the moon by the end of the decade.

Neil Armstrong and Buzz Aldrin made that landing on July 20, 1969, and I remember it as if it were yesterday. That feat has influenced so much of what we do today.

Though space travel was in its infancy, Kennedy's goal ignited NASA and its scientists into action in a way that nothing else could. He plainly said this would happen by the decade's end. He gave us a deadline, without which I doubt we would have seen a moon landing for 20 years or more. All of those who worked on the project felt galvanized to accomplish what had been set forth for them. The setting of a goal fueled their spirits and encouraged them to imagine the possibilities and pursue their potential.

A POWERFUL TOOL

The government knows a lot about deadlines. You get your taxes finished because the government sets the deadline every year at April 15. Local governments set deadlines for road construction crews and usually offer monetary incentives if they can beat those deadlines.

We all face deadlines in our jobs and our daily lives. Newspaper reporters strive to get a story to press by the designated hour. You have to pay your bills on time or face the consequences. When do students usually hand in their homework or study for a test? It is when they realize that the deadline is staring them in the face. In professional sports, when do most of the blockbuster trades take place? You got it: right before the trade deadline.

Think of how much gets done right before you take a vacation. Why? Because you have a deadline. You probably get more done in that final week before you leave on vacation than in the two previous weeks. If it weren't for the last minute, it sometimes seems, nothing would get done.

Deadlines make things happen. They are an essential part of our everyday lives, and the trick is to use them to your business advantage, and in your personal life as well. It is easy to talk about dreams. They may be beautiful, but they are only fluff unless you can turn them into specific goals. By putting a deadline on a dream, you are setting a target for making it come true. "We'll go to Paris someday!" a couple may say over the years, while they grow grizzled and frustrated waiting for that someday to come. You can dream until you die, and where did those dreams take you? You need to set a date and take action to make it happen, and then your dream becomes a lovely memory: "We'll always have Paris!"

HOW TO INSPIRE A CONTRACTOR

I was fixing up a summer home that I needed to sell in a small town in the Midwest. It needed quite an extensive rehab, a new roof, interior painting, floor refinishing, plumbing, and electrical work.

My mother, who owned a house across the street, had contracted to do many of those same things for her own home. The work on her home took six months to complete. How, she asked, was I able to manage to get things done so swiftly that my summer home was ready to sell?

The secret was the power of the deadline. You see, as I met with the various contractors, I emphasized that these projects had to be finished within two weeks or I wouldn't be hiring them or paying them. They all agreed up front to have the work finished in those two weeks. It was work that, ordinarily, would have taken them two months to schedule and finish, but they got it done on my timeline.

A miracle? No, it was the power of the deadline. I am a great believer in assigning deadlines to my employees, suppliers, and projects. The book that you are reading had a deadline. That is a major reason it is here now for you to read. Without the deadline, it might have languished as a project that would be completed sometime in the future. And as we all know, "sometime" can seem to take an eternity.

CONSEQUENCES AND INCENTIVES

It is amazing to me how my office gets cleaned up and organized when I know that I soon will be getting a visit from an important customer. I imagine that you know just what I mean. And if facing a deadline has that effect on you, you can be sure it is a powerful tool to spur productivity among those with whom you deal on the job and through your business.

Without a deadline, goals can become nebulous. People get lazy or they just put a project off as long as possible. So put a deadline on that project. Put a deadline on that supplier delivery. Put a deadline on that service requirement, and let there be consequences if the timeline is not met. If you do not follow up on those deadlines and there are no consequences, you won't get the full benefit of this great tool.

When handing out projects or assignments or goals to your employees, put a deadline on them. Ask your employees by what date and time they will have a task done. Then, throughout the week, let them verbalize to you that they understand the deadline and their commitment to it.

The power of the deadline is one of the most powerful business principles that I know. And when you combine deadline with monetary incentives, it is even more powerful. Customers often are willing to pay extra for a speedy delivery or for the expedited completion of a project. Contractors will work diligently for the premium of meeting an early target date.

Use this principle regularly. If you use it every day, it will take a lot of stress out of managing business and managing life. It helps, whether you are setting deadlines for yourself or for others. Deadlines help us set the pace and avoid those last-minute nightmares.

All those who have planned a wedding, for example, know they need to observe various deadlines along the way, starting months in advance, or the special day could become a stress fest.

Anyone who has arrived late for a flight at the airport understands the consequences of missed deadlines and failing to figure in time for contingencies.

You'll do well to apply that lesson to all your business and personal pursuits. Try it. Do it. It works!

"Change is vital, improvement
the logical form of change."

—JAMES CASH PENNEY

(who succeeded without a degree)

....

CHAPTER 8

NO END TO IMPROVEMENT

I n 1979, the Ford Motor Company produced a car model with transmissions from two sources: the United States and Japan. Very soon after the model was introduced, customers began asking for the Japanese transmission instead of the American-made transmission. They were even willing to wait longer to get the one from Japan.

Even though both transmissions were made to the same specifications, the Japanese transmissions worked better. Intrigued and puzzled, the Ford engineers disassembled the Japanese transmission and discovered something very interesting. The American and Japanese transmissions looked the same, but the engineer's scrutiny revealed that the Japanese parts were held to much tighter tolerances. The parts had about half the permitted tolerance of their American counterparts. Thus, the Japanese transmissions ran more smoothly and experienced less problems.

This discovery led the Ford Motor Company to a man who was a superstar on the subject of quality management in Japan but little known here in the United States. His name was W. Edwards Deming.

Deming, born in Iowa, was recruited by Ford in 1981 to help resolve its quality problems. Ford had lost $3 billion between 1979 and 1982. Deming brought in a whole new mindset to quality management and reintroduced statistical analysis. You can read about Deming and his work in his groundbreaking book *Out of the Crisis*. It is a classic to this day and presents Deming's 14 points that constitute his theory of quality management. His new quality culture helped Ford to improve its quality reputation immensely and become the most profitable American auto company by 1986.

Japan had to deliver the American auto industry a hard slap to the head. Why? Because here in America the automobile manufacturers had fallen asleep at the wheel and believed the mantra that they were "good enough," even as our cars were rusting away underneath us as we drove them to the junk yards.

A MAJOR IMPROVEMENT

I remember having a 1974 Ford Pinto. It lasted less than four years and 50,000 miles. It literally rusted away in front of my eyes and it was in the repair shop constantly. Contrast that with my 2000 Ford F150 Harley Davidson truck that has way over 200,000 miles and has been virtually trouble-free, despite the rough use I have given it.

Being in the manufacturing and precision machining business myself (www.ejbasler.com), I can attest to the much-improved tolerances and quality standards of the auto industry here in America. There are now quality management certifications that manufacturers can obtain. Among them are the ISO9001 and TS16949 certifications. My company has been ISO9001 certified for many years and recently TS16949 certified. This is one of the highest quality certifications in the world and also the automotive industry's quality management standard. It takes hard work, time, and discipline to obtain these. But if you want to be competitive in a world market and continuously improve, these quality management standards will help you to become the best in your industry.

RISING ABOVE THE MEDIOCRE

One of my favorite TV shows is *Restaurant Impossible*, hosted by Chef Robert Irvine. Each week, he visits a failing restaurant by invitation and gets the opportunity to try to turn it around in five days. Now, we all know that turnarounds do not happen in a week, except on reality TV shows. But Irvine and his team give it their best shot and, sometimes, with surprising results.

Week after week, what hits me in these failing restaurants is that somewhere along the line, the owners settled for "good enough" rather than "best" and got tired of improving their food, menu items, service staff, and décor. Mediocre became the rule of the day, and their businesses began to slowly bleed to death. Being "good enough" puts you on the road to eventual failure.

Like the proverbial frog in the kettle, the owners have no clue what has happened until Irvine comes in and hits them over the head with a few verbal two-by-fours. They hear the harsh truth. How did this happen? No business starts out with the goal of being mediocre. Yet, how often do you walk into a restaurant that has become that way? Sadly, I am sure you have seen far too many.

In every business with which I have been involved, I have had the goal of improving it in every way possible. I seek out feedback to see where we can improve our product, customer service, delivery, and more. Someone once said if you settle for average, you are the best of the lousiest and the lousiest of the best.

Today, you do not have to reinvent the wheel. There are so many resources available to a business owner just on the Internet alone. Yelp, Google Reviews, and Yahoo Reviews are tremendously helpful if you have a food or service company or are a retailer. They provide some very good, free customer feedback if you can accept it without getting overly offended.

Customer surveys and quality ratings are available now from the larger customers in manufacturing. There are tremendous free articles on the web regarding best practices in continuous quality improvement, with the emphasis on continuous. It is not a one-time cure or a quick fix. It is a strategic mindset that is never satisfied with the current quality level.

THE VALUE OF FRESH EYES

There is not one thing you are currently making, serving, building, manufacturing, or cooking that cannot be improved. Do you believe that? If not, invite my team to your business and we can prove it to you. My Fresh Eyes team can come out and recommend ways to improve your business.

Business practices are universal, whether you are in a manufacturing or retail business, or whatever your pursuit. I have learned a lot over the years about what makes sense, and I have met a lot of professionals with plenty of their own expertise. And recently, I decided to put that collective wisdom to use in helping others.

I started a business consulting company, Fresh Eyes Coaching, through which I can pull together my network of experts to help a business, whether it is a manufacturing plant, retail store, bakery, or coffee shop. We help them understand, from a fresh perspective, what they need and how they can improve.

We can also send someone into the company for a few days, either as an undercover customer or as an undercover employee, to gain a valuable, fresh perspective on how things operate. That is why I call it Fresh Eyes Coaching.

Over the years, I have done such consulting informally, as a friend helping friends. In my career, I have gotten to know professionals with expertise in their particular fields. I have come to know general managers, real estate professionals, legal experts, accountants, retail people, and many others.

These are the people on my team whose expertise I can rely upon, and we can assess how a business is doing and what it could do better. For example, I recently visited a new, hip restaurant that had plenty of waitresses but terrible service. I kept thinking, "Man, I could really help the owner of this place."

When a business seeks our help, first we conduct an interview. What is it seeking? What are its needs? Then we put together a proposal. We might suggest that we send in an undercover employee or some undercover customers over the next two weeks. It is not a question of one price fits all. Each business is different, and what we recommend depends on what each business needs. We have a menu of services, which includes a generous helping of meat and potatoes.

Sometimes, all it takes is a set of fresh eyes—or several sets—to look at an operation and help to get things on to a smooth course for growth. I have seen that principle in action through-out my life in many ways, as a businessman, a family man, and a pastor.

I have seen how people need a fresh perspective that will keep them accountable. They need good advice from people who have been down the same road and on roads they have yet to travel. It can be intimidating to launch a business with limited resources and the feeling that your education is inadequate. "I am not some rich guy with an MBA," you might think in a weak moment, "and maybe I am not up to the challenge."

Yes, you are up to the challenge, and if you need some coaching and some encouragement, I want to be there to help. I have a heart for small businesses. I know the dreams and the needs of the entrepreneur, and I understand the spirit. I like to help people fulfill the American dream.

Any business could benefit from having someone new coming in and taking a fresh look and giving some beneficial recommendations. You may need those fresh eyes to get yourself re-inspired. There will be many times you'll need to get yourself re-inspired because business is a marathon, not a sprint. You may find yourself neglecting things you may never have neglected at the start of things or be blinded to problems because you are just too busy or just worn out.

The undercover customers and employees can blend in and observe your operations and can make recommendations to help you become more successful. Experienced fresh eyes can discover many things that are hindering your sales, productivity, profitability, and quality.

We recently helped a restaurant whose owner was bemoaning the fact that he had no customers. The food was very good, but the décor was drab and the menu seemed confusing. Very little marketing was being done. Our team went in and made recommendations for the décor, menu, and marketing. We created an experience, not just a destination for food. Within six months, the business was booming, and the owner was very happy!

Contact us at www.fresheyescoaching.com for more information.

A NEW PERSPECTIVE

When my son-in-law first came into our manufacturing business, we had him report to us the things he saw before everyone knew he was part of the family. He looked at things far differently from the way we had become accustomed to seeing and accepting them. The changes we have made in the past few years have been a direct result of his early experiences and observations.

One of the things that he saw was how some employees outperformed others who were running the same machines but on different shifts. That led us to publicly post our production values as a way to motivate underperforming employees to increase their production.

We run 24 hours a day here. When I first brought my son-in-law in, I put him on the third shift, right on the line. He noticed that the third-shift guys were outperforming the second- and first-shift guys by 30 percent. That opened our eyes and led us to wonder what the reason for that might be. Was it because there are fewer distractions that late at night? Whatever the reason, my son-in-law noticed the discrepancy immediately. We started posting people's production publicly on our boards, and nobody wanted to be at the bottom of the totem pole.

He also noticed that some of the parts we were producing were consistently having to be 100 percent inspected before they were shipped to customers. Normally, you shouldn't have to inspect 100 percent to ensure quality, and it adds extra labor and costs. Having to inspect 100 percent indicates there has to be a better way to make the part. His observation led us to come up with better manufacturing processes, which greatly improved our product quality results.

MY FAVORITE STORE

A grocery store chain called Mariano's recently started operating in the Chicago area and is taking the grocery store experience to a new level. It is run by CEO Bob Mariano. It has the competition running scared. Already, the second largest grocery chain in Chicago has closed its stores.

When you walk into Mariano's stores, you are not only there to buy groceries, you are there to have a great experience in food, service, quality, and variety. The stores offer everything from a European flower experience to take-away meat grilled over charcoal to a bakery that leaves others to shame. They have freshly squeezed juices, amazing fruit and salad bars, a café and restaurant, and other amenities.

But what really sets Mariano's stores apart is their quality and commitment to an excellent customer experience. The Jewel and the Dominick's chains owned the market for over 50 years, but they fell asleep at the wheel. The stores were dirty and understaffed with little in the way of innovations or uniqueness. They were nondescript and uninspiring. Mariano's stores have also been a wake-up call to Whole Foods, which has largely been unrivaled for the last 15 years here. Along comes Bob Mariano and his stores, and it is a game changer. I was in their first store in 2010 and, from day one, I was amazed at the difference in my buying experience,

Mariano now has 25 stores and soon will have 50 stores, just in the Chicago area. The chain has differentiated itself for a competitive advantage.

Ask yourself what makes your business different from dozens of your competitors. What will be your competitive advantage in the marketplace? Price, quality, uniqueness, customer service, exceptional value, expertise? Is there one factor you can emphasize that will really make you different?

I recently was driving through the South Side of Chicago and came upon a street where there recently had been a dozen small diners and fast food restaurants within a three-block span. Only three were still in business. Why? Because those three figured out their competitive advantage. The other nine restaurants, upon closer examination, all had looked the same and had virtually the same food products and prices.

WHAT BRINGS THE CUSTOMER BACK?

Realize that on any given day your competition is working on improving what you currently provide to your customers. They are studying you as we speak, and they are figuring out a way to capture your customers. How do you fight back? You fight back with the quality mindset that there is no end to improving your products and service.

Tom Peters had this observation after he had researched, over the years, some of the best companies in the world. "Excellent firms do not believe in excellence, only in constant improvement and constant change." You must always keep on learning, and you must grow your quality systems or die—a simple truth.

Edwards Deming once said that "profit in business comes from repeat customers that boast about your product or service and that bring friends with them."

You won't have a successful business without repeat customers and you won't have repeat customers if you do not have a quality product and superior customer service. You want your customers to recommend you to their peers, friends, neighbors, and other people in their company or other divisions in their company. Why not set your goal to be the best in your industry, whatever business you are in?

> "Your time is limited, so do not waste it living someone else's life."
>
> —STEVE JOBS
>
> *(who succeeded without a degree)*

....

SIMPLE AND HEARTY

From the days of Ben Franklin to Steve Jobs, America has long been a land of pioneers and entrepreneurs. And yes, the American dream is still alive and this is proven every single day.

Today, as in generations past, people from many other countries have come here with much desire, hope, and vision. They start out with virtually nothing, but succeed greatly.

I think of my friends Ted and Lisa from Greece, who run the L&L Snack Shop in Des Plaines, Illinois. They came here with very little, took over a struggling storefront restaurant and turned it into one of the best breakfast diners in Chicago and, at the same time, put four kids through college.

I think of Adolfo from Mexico who now runs a very successful fencing and landscaping company.

These are just two among the tens of thousands of stories of immigrants succeeding in business. I would like to hear your story. You can send it through our website at www.meatandpotatoes.com.

EFFORT, NOT EXCUSES

So many people try to come up with excuses. "I do not have enough money," some say, or, "I am not the right race." They talk themselves into believing that they can never get ahead. In fact, statistics show that Americans born in the United States are only half as likely to start businesses as immigrants.

The principles I have laid out here can be applied by anyone running a small business. But there is one more principle I want to share. It is one that my dad instilled in me from the time I could walk, up until his death. It is the principle of hard work with a good attitude.

I watched my dad working in a hot factory, covered in sweat, his clothes oil stained, as he unloaded 12-foot steel bars off flat-bed trucks without the benefit of an overhead crane. I watched him load these bars by hand into machines, without the benefit of a forklift.

I watched him run complicated machinery without the benefit of proper training. I watched him figure out complicated machining problems without the benefit of an engineering degree.

I watched him bless and take good care of his employees. And I watched him model the American dream before my eyes. I am forever grateful and forever inspired.

Running a successful business is hard work. There are no ifs, ands, or buts about that. Many of today's business gurus espouse the idea that hard work is an out-of-date concept. Perhaps it is for some, but for the average small businessman and the hundreds of business owners I have known, the reality is quite different. The most successful people I know are also the hardest workers I know.

Whether you are a businessman, athlete, musician, educator, or salesperson, you know there are no shortcuts to becoming the best. Yes, we must work smarter. I understand that perfectly, but I am not going to let you think that entrepreneurship is an easy road. They say it takes 10,000 hours of practice to become an expert in most fields.

My dad taught me that the easy road eventually leads to poverty and hard work and working smarter will cure a lot of psychiatric and depression problems. I see people sitting at home having pity parties, wasting their hours away, and burying their God-given gifts. Antidepressants cannot cure lack of vision and laziness, but hard work and vision can cure depression and a host of other maladies. Man was created and wired to succeed in a hard world. It takes courage to pursue a dream.

Today, make a vow to stop making excuses. Get up and pursue the dream of entrepreneurship. Experience the amazing feeling of having control over your own destiny. The feeling of empowerment, responsibilities, purpose, and fulfillment all provide an excitement that energizes and reenergizes an entrepreneur. Many of you desire to be your own boss. Go for it, and apply the common-sense principles that will put food on your table. They are the meat and potatoes of business success, delicious and satisfying.

TAKING THAT RISK

Ron Wayne was one of Apple's three cofounders. He was present at the birth of Apple along with Steve Jobs and Steve Wozniak. He designed the company's original logo, wrote the manual for the Apple 1 computer and put together the new partnership agreement that gave him a 10 percent stake in Apple.

In his autobiography, *iWoz*, Wozniak recalls meeting Wayne and thinking, "Wow, this guy is amazing ... He seemed to know all the things we did not." He played a major role in those early days. However, Wayne was risk averse, due to a business failure five years earlier. Twelve days after he signed the agreement for 10 percent of Apple stock, he decided that the wild spending of a young Steve Jobs wasn't worth the risk. He sold his shares back to Apple for $800. Today those shares would be worth $22 billion.

To be a successful entrepreneur, you have to take risks. Entrepreneurship is not for the faint of heart. During different times in my life, I have taken risks. Some have worked out well, and some have not, but I have never had to look back with regret at not trying something because I was afraid.

THE POWER OF LAUGHTER

You need to have to have a sense of humor. Your business is important, but it is just a part of your life—your family, friends, relationships. It is great to be a hard worker and to come home proud of yourself at day's end, but it is more important to have something to come home for.

Things can always get messy with people. Life and work with others is never perfect. Even in the best teams, something will be wrong. You can expect it, so do not take yourself so seriously that you cease to enjoy your life.

Studies show that humor is not only good for your physical health but also good for your mental health. Laughter eases stress, helps you relax and recharge, and helps you shift perspectives. You'll see situations in a less threatening and more realistic light, and when you do, you will be able to make better business decisions. Anger and stress diminish your ability to make good decisions.

My brothers and I will often laugh and find humor at stressful or seemingly overwhelming business problems just to keep our wits and to keep things in perspective. Laughter works.

STRIKING THE RIGHT BALANCE

You have to have balance in your life. It is often said that no one lying on his deathbed wishes he would have spent one more day at the office. It is very important to pace yourself and not burn out. There have been many decisions I would have made in a better way if I had taken a rest and gotten perspective.

Family and friends cannot be neglected en route to your entrepreneurial dream. Every person I know who sacrificed family for business later regretted the decision. I know some executives now who have also decided to turn off their e-mails, computers, and smart phones on Sundays to give themselves a rest and to rejuvenate.

Being "on" for every hour of every day benefits no one. Pushing yourself past your limits will only lead to poor heath, addictions, and bad decisions. You could eventually destroy the business you've worked so hard to build.

The preceding chapters have not been meant to be an all-inclusive how-to book for running a business. Instead, I have given you a guide to those underlying business principles that have been proven to help any type of business to survive and grow and be profitable. That is why you have been reading about vision, having mentors, being a leader, watching important measures, being involved and hands-on, and understanding accounting.

We have taken a look at the importance of hiring well and firing when necessary, and of buying and negotiating effectively. I have explained how checklists and deadlines can dramatically improve productivity, and I have challenged you to grow your business through quality and innovation.

Those are the basics that lay a solid foundation on which you can build your business. They are nothing fancy or complicated. They are not a lot of smoke and mirrors or the high-sounding fads of modern business psychology. The foundation they build is just the nourishing meal that you need right now.

As the good book says: "Be doers of the Word, not just hearers only, deceiving yourselves." Here is your meal, simple and hearty. It will give you the energy you need for action. It is the meal of meat and potatoes for the entrepreneur. Enjoy.

APPENDIX 1

A BRIEF LIST OF SUCCESSFUL PEOPLE
WITHOUT COLLEGE DEGREES

- Walt Disney, *Founder of Disney Studios*

- Steve Jobs, *Co-Founder of Apple*

- Bill Gates, *Billionaire Co-Founder of Microsoft*

- Ray Kroc, *Founder of McDonald's*

- John D. Rockefeller, *Billionaire Founder of Standard Oil*

- Henry Ford, *Founder of Ford Motor Co.*

- Ralph Lauren, *Billionaire Fashion Designer*

- Richard Branson, *Billionaire Founder of Virgin Airlines and Music*

- Marc Zuckerberg, *Billionaire Founder of Facebook*

- Wilbur Wright, *Inventer of the Airplane*

- Ted Turner, *Billionaire Founder of CNN and TBS*

- Mark Twain, *Author*

- Colonel Harlan Sanders, *Founder of KFC*

- Vidal Sassoon, *Founder of Vidal Sassoon*

- David Oreck, *Founder of the Oreck Vacuum Co.*

- J. Paul Getty, *Billionaire Oilman*

- Michael Dell, *Founder of Dell Computers*

- George Eastman, *Inventor and Founder of Kodak*

- Winston Churchill, *British Prime Minister*

- John Mackey, *Founder of Whole Foods*

- Larry Page, *Billionaire Founder of Google*

- Jack Crawford Taylor, *Billionaire Founder of Enterprise Rent-a-Car*

- Andrew Carnegie, *Industrialist and Philanthropist*

This is an abridged list that could contain thousands of well-known names and millions of unknown names who were successful without a degree. It can be done!

APPENDIX 2

THE 20 MOST IMPORTANT INTERVIEW QUESTIONS

1. What are your strengths?

2. What are your weaknesses?

3. Why are you interested in working us?

4. Where do you see yourself
    in 5 years? 10 years?

5. Why do you want to leave
    your current company?

6. What can you offer us that
    someone else can not?

7. Tell me about an accomplishment
    you are most proud of.

8. Tell me about a time you made a mistake.

9. Tell me how you handled a difficult situation.

10. Why should we hire you?

11. Why are you looking for a new job?

12. Would you work weekends/holidays?

13. What are your salary requirements?

14. What was your biggest failure?

15. What are your career goals?

16. What would your boss say if I called your boss right now and asked him what an area that you could improve on is?

17. Are you a leader or a follower?

18. What are some of your leadership experiences?

19. Would you work 40+ hours a week?

20. What questions do you have for me?

APPENDIX 3

The following article was retrieved from the New York State Office of Mental Health website, www.omh.ny.gov/index.html.

TOP TEN INTERNAL CONTROLS TO PREVENT AND DETECT FRAUD!

A recent "KPMG Fraud Survey" found that organizations are reporting more experiences of fraud than in prior years and that three out of four organizations have uncovered fraud. The NYS Office of Mental Health's Bureau of Audit has provided the following list of internal controls to assist you in preventing and detecting fraud at your agency.

1. Use a system of checks and balances to ensure no one person has control over all parts of a financial transaction.

- Require purchases, payroll, and disbursements to be authorized by a designated person.

- Separate handling (receipt and deposit) functions from record keeping functions (recording transactions and reconciling accounts).

- Separate purchasing functions from payables functions.

- Ensure that the same person isn't authorized to write and sign a check.

- When opening mail, endorse or stamp checks "For Deposit Only" and list checks on a log before turning them over to the person responsible for depositing receipts. Periodically reconcile the incoming check log against deposits.

- Require supervisors to approve employees' time sheets before payroll is prepared.

- Require paychecks to be distributed by a person other than the one authorizing or recording payroll transactions or preparing payroll checks.

- If the agency is so small that you can't separate duties, require an independent check of work being done, for example, by a board member.

- Require accounting department employees to take vacations.

2. Reconcile agency bank accounts every month.

- Require the reconciliation to be completed by an independent person who doesn't have bookkeeping responsibilities or check signing responsibilities or require supervisory review of the reconciliation.

- Examine canceled checks to make sure vendors are recognized, expenditures are related to agency business, signatures are by authorized signers, and endorsements are appropriate.

- Examine bank statements and cancelled checks to make sure checks are not issued out of sequence.

- Initial and date the bank statements or reconciliation report to document that a review and reconciliation was performed and file the bank statements and reconciliations.

3. Restrict use of agency credit cards and verify all charges made to credit cards or accounts to ensure they were business-related.

- Limit the number of agency credit cards and users.

- Establish a policy that credit cards are for business use only; prohibit use of cards for personal purposes with subsequent reimbursement.

- Set account limits with credit card companies or vendors.

- Inform employees of appropriate use of the cards and purchases that are not allowed.

- Require employees to submit itemized, original receipts for all purchases.

- Examine credit card statements and corresponding receipts each month, independently, to determine whether charges are appropriate and related to agency business.

4. Provide Board of Directors oversight of agency operations and management.

- Monitor the agency's financial activity on a regular basis, comparing actual to budgeted revenues and expenses.

- Require an explanation of any significant variations from budgeted amounts.

- Periodically review the check register or general ledger to determine whether payroll taxes are paid promptly.

- Document approval of financial procedures and policies and major expenditures in the board meeting minutes.

- Require independent auditors to present and explain the annual financial statements to the Board of Directors and to provide management letters to the Board.

- Evaluate the Executive Director's performance annually against a written job description.

- Participate in the hiring/approval to hire consultants including the independent auditors.

5. Prepare all fiscal policies and procedures in writing and obtain Board of Directors approval. Include policies and/or procedures for the following:

- cash disbursements

- attendance and leave

- expense and travel reimbursements

- use of agency assets

- purchasing guidelines

- petty cash

- conflicts of interest

6. Ensure that agency assets such as vehicles, cell phones, equipment, and other agency resources are used only for official business.

- Examine expense reports, credit card charges, and telephone bills periodically to determine whether charges are appropriate and related to agency business.

- Maintain vehicle logs, listing the dates, times, mileage or odometer readings, purpose of the trip, and name of the employee using the vehicle.

- Periodically review the logs to determine whether usage is appropriate and related to agency business.

- Maintain an equipment list and periodically complete an equipment inventory.

7. Protect petty cash funds and other cash funds.

- Limit access to petty cash funds. Keep funds in a locked box or drawer and restrict the number of employees who have access to the key.

- Require receipts for all petty cash disbursements with the date, amount received, purpose or use for the funds, and name of the employee receiving the funds listed on the receipt.

- Reconcile the petty cash fund before replenishing it.

- Limit the petty cash replenishment amount to a total that will require replenishment at least monthly.

- Keep patient funds separate from petty cash funds.

8. Protect checks against fraudulent use.

- Prohibit writing checks payable to cash.

- Deface and retain voided checks.

- Store blank checks in a locked drawer or cabinet, and limit access to the checks.

- Require that checks are to be signed only when all required information is entered on them and the documents to support them (invoices, approval) are attached.

- Require two signatures on checks above a specified limit. Require board member signature for the second signature above a higher specified limit. (Ensure that blank checks are not pre-signed.)

- Mark invoices "Paid" with the check number when checks are issued.

- Enable hidden flags or audit trails on accounting software.

9. Protect cash and check collections.

- Ensure that all cash and checks received are promptly recorded and deposited in the form originally received.

- Issue receipts for cash, using a pre-numbered receipt book.

- Conduct unannounced cash counts.

- Reconcile cash receipts daily with appropriate documentation (cash reports, receipt books, mail tabulations, etc.)

- Centralize cash receipts whenever possible.

10. Avoid or discourage related party transactions.

- Require that a written conflict of interest and code of ethics policy is in place and that it is updated annually.

- Require that related party transactions be disclosed and be approved by the Board.

- Require competitive bidding for major purchases and contracts.

- Discourage the hiring of relatives and business transactions with Board members and employees.

CPSIA information can be obtained
at www.ICGtesting.com
Printed in the USA
LVHW031039100220
646400LV00004B/533